Cultural Identity
and the Nation-State

Cultural Identity and the Nation-State

Edited by
Carol C. Gould and Pasquale Pasquino

ROWMAN & LITTLEFIELD PUBLISHERS, INC.
Lanham • Boulder • New York • Oxford

ROWMAN & LITTLEFIELD PUBLISHERS, INC.

Published in the United States of America
by Rowman & Littlefield Publishers, Inc.
4720 Boston Way, Lanham, Maryland 20706
www.rowmanlittlefield.com

12 Hid's Copse Road
Cumnor Hill, Oxford OX2 9JJ, England

British Library Cataloguing in Publication Information Available

Library of Congress Cataloging-in-Publication Data

Cultural identity and the nation-state / Carol C. Gould and Pasquale Pasquino, editors.
   p. cm.
  ISBN 0-8476-9676-6 (alk. paper)—ISBN 0-8476-9677-4 (pbk. : alk. paper)
   1. Minorities. 2. State, The. 3. Nationalism. 4. Ethnicity. 5. Multiculturalism. 6.
  Citizenship. I. Gould, Carol, 1946– II. Pasquino, Pasquale, 1948–

JC312 .C85 2001
323.1—dc21

00-051814

Printed in the United States of America

⊗™ The paper used in this publication meets the minimum requirements of American
National Standard for Information Sciences—Permanence of Paper for Printed Library
Materials, ANSI/NISO Z.39.48–1992.

Contents

Preface

The affirmation of cultural difference, the resurgence of nationalism and religious fundamentalism, and new emphases on ethnicity, together with the emergence of economic and political globalization, have created sharp problems for older conceptions of citizenship and universal rights within democratic societies. This book considers current philosophical and political arguments concerning alternative conceptions of cultural and national identity, as well as the theoretical conflicts that have emerged about pluralism and multiculturalism within nation-states, rights for minority cultures, and national self-determination. Several of the essays focus on alternative models of cultural diversity and the issue of state support for culture in general and for minority cultures in particular. A related theme is the tension between the recognition of diverse cultures, on the one hand, and of cosmopolitan or universal frameworks of human rights, on the other. The question is addressed whether new norms or values, along with new forms of governance, are required in this current context. The role of democratic and civic institutions is also scrutinized here, as is the function of constitutional adjudication for contemporary democracies.

Several authors explicitly reflect on United States, Canadian, and French perspectives on these issues, since policies and practices with respect to cultural identity have recently come under especially sharp scrutiny in public debate in those countries, with competing models for the treatment of immigrants and cultural minorities among their citizenry. Yet, the considerations raised clearly have an impact on democratic states generally, particularly in the current context of globalization, insofar as these societies attempt to maintain universalist traditions of justice and rights, while giving new weight to the diversity of cultures within them. Economic, technological, and political globalization introduce new complexities into this situation, not only by establishing global interconnections between heretofore more self-contained cultures and regions but also by extending commercialization and a certain homogenization, even of cultural traditions, worldwide. This distinctive intersection of democracy, globalization, and cosmopolitan frameworks of rights poses new questions about recognizing cultural identities and the scope of national or political communities, which in turn prompts some of the reflections and analyses collected here.

Among the issues addressed in this volume are the following:

- Multicultural versus integrationist approaches to ethnic differences in matters of language, education, and the support of culture more generally. Is cultural pluralism always required, or is there a role for a national culture?
- Different models of the assimilation of immigrants and their rights. Furthermore, are the requirements for recognizing native groups with their own institutional forms of self-governance different from such requirements for immigrant groups?
- The meaning of self-determination, and the basis and scope of this idea. What is the significance of an individual's right to cultural expression and development in this context? Do new forms of political or ecological cooperation give rise to a new interpretation of self-determination beyond the limits of nation-states? What are the limits of rights to national self-determination?
- Is the unity of a nation-state found in its prepolitical community or in its political constitution as a state, and what is the impact of this for issues of the self-determination of peoples? What is the role of a constitution in setting the framework for democratic decision making, and how is this role understood in various contemporary nation-states?
- How can democratic states cope with the dual and apparently contrasting problems posed by religious fundamentalisms and by the increasing role given to market relations that the global economy produces? What are the new opportunities and also the new problems for democratic governance that are posed by increasing economic and political globalization?
- How can one deal with oppressive cultural practices that may violate human rights—for example, female genital mutilation? What is the role of universal conceptions of human being in grounding the human rights and in permitting a critique of such practices?
- Does the state have an obligation to support culture generally and, in that case, also the diverse cultures of ethnic minorities? Can it do so in a fair way that does not violate its neutrality or basic standards of democratic procedure? Is a tyranny of the majority culture(s) inevitable within nation-states?

- What are the relations among cultural identity, ethnicity, and nationality? What is the import of recent globalization processes for recognizing cultural identity and ethnicity within the framework of nation-states? Are there new forms of citizenship that are appropriate in this context?

With essays by philosophers and political theorists from the United States, Canada, and France, this volume takes up these largely new and difficult questions concerning cultural identity in the nation-state. Although significant theoretical analyses of these questions already appear in the literature, several of the essays in this collection argue in various ways against the grain, representing distinctive approaches to self-determination, multiculturalism, individual and group rights, and the relation of these to a constitutional framework and to a democratic civil society. The essays tend to proceed by reviewing alternative positions and arguing in rather dialectical ways for positions that reconcile the conflicting views and preserve the strengths of the existing alternatives in plausible new syntheses.

The first topic in the collection is the idea of self-determination. In what sense should it be given moral weight? In his essay "The Ethics of Self-Determination: Democratic, National, Regional," Omar Dahbour argues that this idea has played an important, if problematic, role in recent debates about the ethics of international relations. He notes its historical importance in nineteenth-century demands for statehood of European nationalities, followed by the national liberation struggles in the colonial world during the early twentieth century and, in more contemporary terms, in the moves toward secession by certain national groups. Yet, despite its political importance, self-determination in Dahbour's view has some morally troubling dimensions. He regards it as an ambiguous concept that is to a degree compatible with the major tendencies in recent international law and ethics but in other ways undercuts those same tendencies. His essay distinguishes three different interpretations of this principle of self-determination, which he calls democratic, national, and regional. While Dahbour endorses the democratic interpretation, he notes some of its limitations. He criticizes one prominent philosophical justification for the national interpretation of this principle that he calls the "right to culture" argument. He then argues for what he calls a regional principle of self-determination, which bases it in an ecologically-defined conception of community, and notes some implications of adopting this principle for various issues in international, environmental, and business ethics.

Christopher W. Morris, in his "Peoples, Nations, and the Unity of Societies," takes up the perplexing question of what makes a society one. He questions the common view in Enlightenment cultures such as those of the United States or France that the unity of a culture cannot depend on preexisting social ties—for example, those of nationality, feelings of community, or religious faiths—without those states losing their universalism. This position is identified in the American case with the writings of Thomas Jefferson, but, according to Morris, Jefferson

does not in fact hold that the unity of a society is independent of the particular social relationships or ties of members but rather thinks that distinct peoples should
be allowed independence. For Morris, Enlightenment states can maintain their
contemporary cosmopolitan self-image only by disregarding the "protonationalism" evident in Jefferson. In his conclusion, Morris defends the idea that a commitment to (certain) universal rights of persons is compatible with understanding
the unity of societies to be at least partly based on particular social relations, including those of a national sort.

In his essay "Could Canada Turn into Bosnia?" the philosopher Frank Cunningham observes how philosophers and political theorists attempting to understand national conflicts typically address a standard group of questions—the definition of "nation"; the relations among individual, national, and subnational
group rights; democracy and nationhood; nationalism and globalism—and adopt
well-defined stances from which to make their prescriptions—for instance, from
the standpoint of liberal individualism, communitarianism, or political realism.
Considering the example of the national conflict between Anglo Canadians and
Franco Quebecers, his essay maintains that when the situation of the first nations
(or native Canadians) is taken politically into account (as is also happening elsewhere), the questions and standard answers to them, as well as the prescriptive
stances, are inadequate and need reinterpretation. This is partly due to the unique
political and moral challenges presented by land claims and other requirements
for transgenerational redress and partly because notions like "sovereignty,"
"right," and "democracy" in aboriginal usage strain nonaboriginal attempts at
conceptual and political accommodation. Cunningham suggests that this point
becomes especially relevant in the context of contemporary violent conflicts of
an ethnic or national sort.

How can contemporary democratic governments hold together multicultural
nations? In his "Blood Brothers, Consumers, or Citizens? Three Models of
Identity—Ethnic, Commercial, and Civic," Benjamin R. Barber suggests that
democracy itself provides a way of dealing with multiculturalism by emphasizing civic identity as an extension of democratic membership—that is, citizenship.
Especially in the United States, commitment to constitutional principles, along
the lines of Habermas's "constitutional patriotism," plays a role in uniting people
otherwise divided by private faith, race, gender, class, or ethnic origins. Yet, Barber notes that in recent years the underlying conditions on which the effectiveness of constitutional commitment depend have eroded. Along the lines pursued
in his well-known book *Jihad versus McWorld*, Barber observes that two powerful rivals for identity have tended to overwhelm that of the citizen: a renewed
tribalism or "blood brotherhood," on the one hand, and a postmodern commercial
identity, on the other hand, in which people are taken as consumers, in the context of economic, technological, and market forces that demand integration and
uniformity. He calls this latter context a "McWorld," tied together by communications, information, entertainment, and commerce. Barber argues that these two

alternative identities share an anarchic absence of common will or of conscious and collective human control under the guidance of law—in short, democracy. By contrast, Barber calls for a foundation for civic unity that is fully compatible with democracy. This would constitute a "third way . . . between private markets and coercive government, between anarchistic individualism and dogmatic tribal communitarianism," which he finds in the public space of a civil society.

The issue of the potential conflict between recognizing diverse cultural practices and universalistic standards of human rights or democracy in a cosmopolitan or global context poses difficult normative problems for political philosophy. For example, how can we avoid cultural relativism without imposing universalistic standards on other cultures? In "Two Concepts of Universality and the Problem of Cultural Relativism," Carol C. Gould considers the recent efforts of philosophers such as Martha Nussbaum and Amartya Sen to propose universalistic conceptions of human beings and their properties or capabilities in place of views that emphasize differences in cultures or gender. These proposals in turn permit us to criticize cultural practices that may be oppressive to women or to deal with the problem of persistent poverty in less developed countries. Gould is critical of abstractly universalist conceptions of human beings that remain overtly essentialist in their willingness to specify a determinate list of human characteristics. She notes the older criticism that such views may in fact be historically and culturally biased by deriving their characteristics from dominant groups. She argues further that, when put forward as a basis for development and for human rights, such views may in fact import Western liberal conceptions of norms of development and rights under the guise of the universally human. In the second part of her essay, Gould contrasts this essentialist understanding of universality with an alternative conception of "concrete universality" that advances a more social account of norms, in which they are understood as intercultural creations. Yet, she goes on to suggest how the latter conception can nonetheless leave room for traditionally universalist norms such as the equal freedom recognized by democratic societies and the human rights.

In "The French Republic and the Claims of Diversity," Catherine Audard takes up the central issue of how much a modern state needs to recognize the diverse cultures within it and how it can do so. She focuses on the French conception of *laïcité* (roughly, secularism), which is often criticized for illiberalism and a rejection of the claims of diversity. She questions how valid such criticisms are and whether they withstand a more nuanced view of the nature and purposes of this conception. Audard goes on to ask how *laïcité* can be adapted to the new social and cultural realities of multiethnicity. Her answer is based on a concept of citizenship and its moral standing. Citizenship, for Audard, requires membership in an ethical community, not only integration into a nation-state. In this context, she discusses the issue of the prohibition on Muslim girls wearing the *hidjab,* or veils, in French schools. She suggests that the debate about the hidjab has focused only on the potential split of the French nation into many ethnic groups, bypassing the

question of the needs of the individual for recognition and moral development
through cultural, social, or religious memberships. Audard observes that the centralized state feels threatened by minority cultures and wants to enforce their allegiance and their assimilation into the dominant culture. In the construction of a
French citizenry through secular education, the purposes of assimilation and of
the formation of "good citizens" tend to override simple toleration and basic respect for individual rights. Against that, Audard argues that diversity needs to be
seen as a moral need, not only a threat, and is fostered by the very nature of moral
identity and the self. She proposes that this has to be acknowledged in a new and
richer concept of citizenship within what she calls "the civic nation."

James A. Cohen, in "Value Judgments and Political Assessments about National Models of Citizenship: The U.S. and French Cases," continues these reflections by observing that national models of citizenship are often perceived by
outsiders in ways that deform their premises and the specific ways in which they
function in practice. He takes up two examples: perceptions of the French republican model of citizenship by foreign observers, in particular North Americans,
and perceptions of the United States model by French observers. He proposes
first that the French republican model of citizenship is not always clearly understood by observers abroad: the constraints it places on the cultural, linguistic, and
religious practices of immigrants are less severe and less "assimilationist" than
they are taken to be. The multiculturalist perspective of many foreign observers
makes it difficult for them to see that the French model is not inconsistent with
full tolerance of cultural practices in the private sphere, with "intercultural" policies in the public sphere, and with certain forms of positive or affirmative action,
so long as they do not refer explicitly to the ethnic or national origins of bene-
ficiaries. In an analogous way, from the French republican point of view, the
United States model of citizenship is often designated as the very example of
what to avoid (i.e., the fragmentation of society into ethnic communities that
crystallize into political blocs). Starting from this premise, certain French observers take a dim view of any kind of practice involving positive or affirmative
action and tend to make value judgments about the United States that are not
founded in an understanding of how affirmative action and discourses of multiculturalism function in the U.S. political context. Cohen advocates, in conclusion,
a more historicized and contextualized understanding of each national model of
citizenship—an attitude that would not preclude value judgments about these
models but that would make for more circumspect judgments, grounded in the
politically possible.

In the final chapter, "Constitutional Adjudication and Democracy," Pasquale
Pasquino also uses a comparative perspective, drawing on the United States,
France, and Italy to elucidate the important issue of the relation of constitutional courts and democratic decision making in modern nation-states. Because of the role of independent constitutional courts, Pasquino notes that a
constitutional democracy or state may be understood as one in which the will

of an elected majority can in fact be struck down or modified—at least for a time—by an unelected body that is politically unaccountable. Pasquino takes up the apparent conflict that this poses with democratic values and beliefs, suggesting that a new doctrine of limited government—a postdemocratic rather than a predemocratic one—becomes central for contemporary political theory. The American institution of judicial review is specifically compared with the constitutional court systems that emerged in Germany, Italy, and France only in the middle of the twentieth century. He concludes that the institutions of a constitutional state cannot be deduced from the single value of democracy alone. In his view, while it is a crucial value, democracy is not the only one that we ought to care about, and perhaps it is not even the one we do care most about in constitutional states. In this chapter, as in the previous two, the use of comparative perspectives helps to clarify current issues on the agenda in the United States and other democratic nation-states.

1

The Ethics
of Self-Determination

Democratic, National, Regional

OMAR DAHBOUR

The idea of self-determination has played an important, if problematic, role in recent debates about the ethics of international relations. Historically, self-determination became important internationally with the demands for statehood of European nationalities in the nineteenth century. It gained additional currency with the rise of struggles for so-called national liberation in the colonial world during the early twentieth century and has retained its global relevance after the success of the anticolonial movements with contemporary calls for secession by national groups in a variety of states.[1]

But despite the political importance of the idea of self-determination in the last two hundred years, it continues to be morally problematic. This is because self-determination is a concept with radically different meanings—ones that can be either compatible or incompatible with other current doctrines in international law and ethics, depending on the meaning that is accepted. This chapter will distinguish these different meanings from one another and determine whether self-determination is indeed an important principle to affirm in contemporary international relations (and in what sense).

What I propose to do here is to distinguish among three different interpretations of a principle of self-determination (which I call the democratic, national, and regional principles), giving some examples of each. In discussing the democratic principle, I will note its limitations, while still endorsing it in some form. Then, I will describe and criticize in some detail a recent philosophical justification for the national principle that I call the "right to culture" argument. Finally, I will advocate a regional principle of self-determination, defining it on the basis of an ecological concept of regions, and note some potential problems with this new principle.

LIMITATIONS OF THE DEMOCRATIC PRINCIPLE

The three different interpretations of self-determination named here can be briefly defined as follows. First, self-determination has meant democratic self-rule by the people of an already existing territory. The clearest case of this is its usage in anticolonial movements in which self-determination meant self-rule by the populations of the colonies. Second, a nationalist interpretation of self-determination indicates advocacy of separate statehood for national groups, whether or not these groups are found within already existing, internationally recognized boundaries. Third, self-determination can be applied to certain contemporary movements for indigenous peoples' rights or for the autonomy of substate regions from central authorities, when these are advocated as a means of remedying the marginalization or exploitation of groups leading ecologically distinctive ways of life.

It is useful to note the precise differences among these three principles. When self-determination is regarded as a democratic principle, it is equivalent to the idea that peoples in already existing political communities ought to participate in their own governance. But when self-determination is understood to apply to national groups, it is not self-rule as such that is at issue—the national principle could be (and is) the basis for demands made against avowedly democratic states—but the boundaries of the unit, entity, or territory within which self-rule is to be exercised.[2] Finally, when self-determination is thought of in regional terms, it indicates an interest in the autonomy necessary to protect and enhance the self-sufficiency and distinctiveness of peoples in particular geographic regions or localities.

The democratic principle of self-determination has come to be accepted as an integral part of international law, at least since the promulgation of the Universal Declaration of Human Rights and the United Nations Charter at the end of the 1940s.[3] This is not to say that there have not been some persistent critics of the adoption of any idea of self-determination. Such critics have generally been suspicious either of the philosophical underpinnings of self-determination per se or of the elasticity of the term, which seems to allow for a variety of misapplications.[4]

Nevertheless, most international jurists have come to view self-determination as justified on the basis of considerations of consistency, in the following sense. The democratic principle constitutes the assertion that, when a political entity of some kind exists, its people ought to be self-governing. This would seem to be a simple extension of the act of recognizing *any* political entities as self-governing—for instance, through treaties or membership in international organizations such as the United Nations.[5] If Britain or France, for instance, are recognized as being legitimate international actors (i.e., independent states), then why not also recognize British Guiana or French West Africa as such, since they are already accorded separate status even by their imperial rulers? Obviously, such an idea was most effectively used to justify the independence of colonies from their colonizers.

Of course, this view begs a question that can only be given cursory notice here: namely, why necessarily accord already existing state boundaries legitimacy? This question tends to come to the fore in philosophical discussions of international relations more than legal ones for the obvious reason that international law assumes the legitimacy of states as its primary claimants.[6] But in various other contexts—for instance, in different interpretations of how to apply Rawlsian hypothetical contract theory to the international realm—the necessary legitimacy of existing states has come into question.[7]

Nevertheless, for our purposes, it is sufficient to assume that if self-determination has *any* legitimate application to international affairs, it is one that, at the very least, accords a right of self-government to all existing states. (It is important to remember here that this—and not a specific type of regime—is what democracy means in the international context.) A final question worth asking about this democratic principle, however, is whether there are any entities to which it is now applicable in the postcolonial era.

One view of how the democratic principle might be extended from a colonial to a postcolonial context is to ensure that, within existing states, no groups or categories of persons are systematically excluded from the same degree of political participation as others. Something like this idea was used to criticize the apartheid regime in South Africa.[8] An even more contemporary case might be that of Palestine.[9] The Palestinian problem raises the issue of whether, when a group lacks political participation within an existing state, it may legitimately claim statehood for itself. This would require some specification of when a group has a kind of *neo*colonial status, about which there is no consensus in international law. But such an idea does not seem to be, prima facie, an illegitimate extension of the democratic principle.

Without committing myself at this point to one or another interpretation of the democratic principle, I simply want to suggest that it is generally recognized today in some form and may have applicability to certain cases in the postcolonial world. It is important to note, however, that its scope, however extended, will still be insufficient either to mollify nationalists who seek new states or to address the concerns of those who seek to preserve regionally distinct ways of life.

This is because, in the first case, the aim of democratic self-determination is to ensure not that particular cultural nations have states of their own but that peoples generally have the right to participate politically in some state. While this view will not satisfy nationalists, I will maintain, for purposes of allowing the cultural expression of different nationalities (often within the same states), that it should.

A second problem, however, is truly unaddressed by the democratic principle—that of the self-determination of indigenous peoples or exploited substate regions that seek to protect or maintain a distinctive society or way of life within a state. This is, of course, a variant of the classic problem of the domination of minorities within a majoritarian political system—but as applied to minorities constituted not by opinion, interest, or nationality but by particular places, needs, or material cultures. This problem is also ignored or even worsened by a nationalist view of self-determination as essentially applicable to groups with distinctive national identities.

Global ethics, just as much as traditional moral and political philosophy, has been affected by a new interest in cultural identity and difference and the norms that supposedly arise from affirmations of specific identities. In fact, international relations was the first arena in which what is today sometimes called multiculturalism, or, more accurately perhaps, identity politics, was formulated.

Nationalism was seen, at least by its advocates, as challenging attempts to develop universal norms of conduct for relations among states and peoples in the international arena. Instead, nationalism, as an assertion of the rights of culturally distinct groups, was regarded as trumping considerations of legal consistency, distributive justice, or human rights. The remainder of this chapter will examine and criticize one aspect of this assertion—a philosophical justification for the principle of national self-determination—and then present an argument for a principle of regional self-determination that may offer a means of remedying problems that the democratic principle truly does not address.[10]

THE NATIONAL PRINCIPLE
AND THE RIGHT TO CULTURE ARGUMENT

National self-determination can be defined as the idea that nationalities may rightfully determine the boundaries, membership, and political status of their own communities, including asserting a right to statehood. The ethical justification of this principle begins from the idea that individuals, as moral agents, have rights to their own well-being. Among the conditions for well-being is the ability to engage in the expression of one's cultural mores, values, and customs. Yet, to do this, one must have a right to engage in cultural expression and to the conditions that allow this. Proponents of the national principle argue that a nation-state is often a necessary condition for the realization of this right.[11] Thus, an ethical justification of the principle can be understood as based on a "right to culture"—namely, as the idea that the right of individuals to express, participate in, and propagate a distinctive culture requires that the cultural groups of which they are members be able to establish independent states within which these activities can be pursued.

In arguing for the idea of self-determination on ethical grounds, philosophers have sought to derive a justification for the principle by establishing a connection between human well-being and particular facts or states of affairs. One such fact or state of affairs is the existence of large groups with distinctive cultures, which Avishai Margalit and Joseph Raz have called "encompassing groups."

What is the significance of such groups? Membership in groups is regarded as important for individuals, since without such membership, their well-being may be adversely affected. For individuals, write Margalit and Raz, membership "greatly affects one's opportunities, one's ability to engage in the relationships and pursuits marked by the culture."[12] Nations are, of course, encompassing groups. So self-determination is based on the idea that encompassing groups are vitally important for the well-being of their members.[13]

Encompassing groups are distinguished by a number of features, including a common character, a particular culture of socialization, the identification of members through a process of "mutual recognition," and a predominant form of personal identity.[14] Given this conception of encompassing groups, the connections between group membership and well-being are twofold. First, the material prosperity of the group tends to be important for the prosperity and flourishing of its members.[15] Second, since individuals' identity is formed in relation to such groups, their sense of themselves—their dignity and self-respect, to use Kantian terms—is inextricably connected with the general reputation or reception of their group.[16]

But the argument for a principle of self-determination not only relies on the claim that there is an important connection between individual well-being and the welfare of encompassing groups (such as nations).[17] It also depends on the idea that self-determination means the "right to decide" about the conditions of well-being for a group. So, even if one might contend that a national group's well-being is not served by a separate state, the group's decision to seek a state is regarded as *sufficient* reason for their claim to be honored.

The reason for this is that, if a claim to self-determination is made dependent on a demonstration of actual oppression or lack of well-being, then the decision to make the claim would become a matter of rational argument or common agreement, not a right of any encompassing group. The idea of *self*-determination would therefore be, in an important sense, unrealized, since its assertion would depend on a demonstration of some prior condition or state and not on the assertion of the claim itself.[18]

What does this "right to decide" amount to? While groups are important to individuals for the cultural context that they provide for socialization, individuation, and mutuality, advocacy of a principle of self-determination suggests that something more is required for groups to provide for the well-being of their members. This additional element is the state—specifically, a nation-state able to provide the adequate cultural context.

The connection between encompassing groups and individual well-being has so far only generated a "right to culture"—a right to be able to participate freely in a group's cultural life. But this doesn't seem to entail a corresponding right to a state. Those philosophers who argue that it does, however, ultimately rely on a belief that state power is essential in order for cultures to flourish.[19]

Why do they think this? The fundamental idea is Hegelian: that it is only through the recognition of others that identity is assured and that the state is necessary for such recognition to be institutionalized, for it to be real, and not simply a moral abstraction.[20] This requirement that the state play a role in ensuring our identity and culture has two aspects.

First, without the state, cultural survival cannot be assured. In certain circumstances, cultural groups may be thought to require an independent state to receive adequate recognition from others.[21] This is especially so today, according to Will Kymlicka, since the only cultures that can escape marginalization are increasingly "societal cultures"—those that can use state institutions to ensure their dominance within a given territory.[22]

But a second aspect of the connection between a right to culture and a right to a state has to do not with cultural survival but with cultural enjoyment.[23] Yael Tamir emphasizes this in arguing that cultures, to be fully enjoyed, must be experienced on a large (national) scale; and this requires the action and cooperation of a state that can organize the distinctive traits of a culture—for example, national holidays, official languages, cultural symbols such as flags or costumes, sports teams able to compete internationally, and so forth.[24] Nations must be able to have states that can ensure that these features of culture are respected, indeed mandated, for a people. A right to a state therefore follows from the interest that individuals have in living within a culture of their choice.[25]

DOES A RIGHT TO CULTURE ENTAIL THE RIGHT TO A STATE?

The basic defect of the right to culture argument is that the real connection between the well-being of individuals and the necessity of nation-states is misunderstood: rather than playing a role in protecting national groups as a context for the development of individual identities, nation-states are actually either irrelevant to the survival of group cultures or harmful to the free self-development of individuals. Nation-states instead contribute mainly to the creation of official cultures that serve the further consolidation of state power.[26]

The concept of encompassing groups on which the ethical justification of the national principle rests assumes the equivalence of personal identities with national identities. Yet, this is surely false. Why, for instance, couldn't some people live a satisfying life in a small-scale community, without having or even wanting membership in a larger encompassing group? Or why couldn't someone see fit to identify with their social class, occupational role, or city or region without feeling at a loss in the absence of ties to a specifically encompassing group?

One answer would be that there is such a thing as "national character" and that, even if it does not subsume all of what we know to be culture, it is nevertheless a very important part of it.[27] But asserting that persons have one (and only one) national identity, and that this identity is readily recognizable, distorts the very processes by which cultures are constituted by presupposing the static and necessary character of cultural differences.[28]

While national identities are undoubtedly a part of the cultural experiences of many individuals, they are not equivalent to cultures in general.[29] Neither are they the stable reference points for individual identities that nationalists assume them to be.[30] Nations, like other cultural groups, are formed from the ascription of one of many potential identities to individuals; they are not the only or even the most obvious context for individuation.[31]

Furthermore, there are ways in which giving nations the right to states may actually restrict and undermine individual self-determination. This is because any particular cultural identity that individuals embody or adopt may only further their own life-plans temporarily or in limited ways. It cannot be assumed that particular national identities will necessarily always serve as the basis for people's self-identification or mutual recognition, especially if such national identities are regarded as excluding cultural syncretism or personal transformation.[32]

Individuals' ability to lead fulfilling lives seems to be best served when they have the maximum opportunity to change their group affiliations and cultural identities in relation to changing needs and interests; it is not only group membership, but individuals' ability to change membership, that is important.[33] This is why, in the principal documents of international human rights law, cultural rights have always been stipulated in individual terms as rights to cultural expression or to the practice of national cultures by individuals. The establishment of nation-states is either irrelevant to the possession of such rights to individual cultural choice or actually injurious to those persons who seek to express cultural traits that do not readily accommodate themselves to the state.

But it may be that it is the enjoyment of cultures rather than their survival that is really at issue. Perhaps it is not enough for persons to see themselves as members of a cultural nationality and as embodying particular practices, customs, languages, and so on, as they choose. A more "heroic" form of cultural identification in which individuals live vicariously through the state may be the true culmination of cultural development.[34]

Historically, and at present, most national cultures have never had states, yet they have existed, and often flourished, sometimes for centuries.[35] What is actually assumed by exponents of the national principle on this basis is the value, not of a national culture, but of a nation-state as the most perfect manifestation of such a culture.

Surely this is a travesty compared to the diversity of actual cultural expression.[36] What, after all, is there to enjoy about official national cultures? Even if military parades and sports competitions excite some of us, they cannot be taken as representative of human culture as a whole. Nation-states actually enhance just those aspects of culture (and only those aspects) that ratify the power of nation-states.

The "unreal universality" of states, as Marx put it, is, on this account, of more importance than the variety of real human cultures.[37]

At this point, a couple of examples might clarify what is at stake in the argument from a right to culture. The case of Quebec may serve as that of a putative nation that is not a state and that purportedly seeks to become a state on the basis of a *general* right to self-determination—that is, a right that is asserted absent any particular injustice or oppression.

If the Québeçois (i.e., French-speaking, or Francophone, Quebecers) desire self-determination—an independent state distinct from Canada—on cultural grounds, this may be because of a belief that their culture will not survive otherwise, or because they lack the enjoyment of their own state culture. But even if the existence of Québeçois culture were threatened—and even if a separate state could ensure its continuation, something that is far from clear—this would not be sufficient warrant for an independent state, since the continued existence of such a culture cannot be simply assumed to benefit or interest many people living there (whether they are Francophone or Anglophone). And the enjoyment of state ceremonies and official games is also not a significant enough benefit to justify political independence, given the probable costs of creating a new state. The case of Quebec, remember, is not necessarily to be understood as a case of cultural oppression by an Anglophone majority but simply one in which a principle of self-determination could be asserted as deemed desirable by the Francophone population.

But there is a paradox in using the importance of encompassing groups for the survival of cultures to justify a *general* principle of self-determination, asserted as of right. On the one hand, if such groups exist and are able to protect their cultures sufficiently to socialize the young, then they would seemingly have no need for a special right of self-determination. On the other hand, if they are unable to propagate their cultural traditions through socialization, they would therefore not be an encompassing group and consequently could not claim a right of self-determination.

A standard response to this paradox would be to argue that groups have such a right when they are persecuted, discriminated against, or oppressed—when particular conditions obtain that disrupt or destroy a group's capacity for cultural expression. But remedial claims of this nature are too weak to support a general principle of national self-determination, since they would only apply in specific cases of oppression or persecution, not generally.[38] This is the reason that Margalit and Raz, for instance, maintain that the persecution of groups *cannot* serve as grounds for a right of self-determination.[39]

What I earlier called the right to decide becomes important here because if self-determination were thought of only as a remedial right, given certain conditions of oppression, then nations would have no right to assert the principle absent such conditions. What is needed in order that the case for a general national principle not collapse is an understanding of that principle that does not depend on specific conditions obtaining; hence, the principle should apply even if no national oppression is occurring. But, to reiterate, if there is no oppression, then why is there a need for a separate state?

Consider a case in which the national principle is justified only remedially—that is, a case of a supposedly oppressed nation, such as Lithuania. If we give up on a general national principle and simply attempt to apply it to oppressed nations, the problem of determining which nations are actually subject to historical injustices arises. (Note that oppression in this case must simply mean the lack of a nation-state, not an inability to engage in particular kinds of cultural expression, something that could be addressed as a violation of human rights according to prevailing international legal doctrine.)

Determining what is a historical injustice—who is illegitimately deprived of a state—is a problem because, as Lea Brilmayer has put it, there is no beginning point, no originally just state of affairs, with which to compare present injustices.[40] So, in the Lithuanian example, often taken as one of the most obvious cases of a legitimate national claim to self-determination, Lithuania is thought to have had just cause as a result of the Soviet annexation of the country in 1940. Yet this annexation was itself an attempt to recover territory lost when the Soviet Union sued for peace with Germany in 1918. Does Lithuania's twenty years of independence legitimate its claim? Or does Russia's wartime loss of a territory it had ruled since 1795 justify its attempt to reassert its territorial integrity? Without good answers to these questions (and, I believe, there are none), national self-determination cannot be justified as a remedy for historical oppression or injustice.

SELF-DETERMINATION, REGIONAL NOT NATIONAL

If the national principle relies on a right to culture, and yet, if a right to culture does not entail the right to a state, then what is left of the basic idea of self-determination? In other words, what legitimate needs are served by this principle? Of course, it may be construed as nothing more than what I earlier called the democratic principle. But is there any other legitimate application of the idea of self-determination? The basic answer to this is that such an idea should mirror the concept of individual or personal self-determination in enabling relevant agents to autonomously determine the conditions for securing their well-being. The issue, of course, is who are the relevant agents. In this case, the agents would have to be groups capable of a collective identity, just as moral self-determination applies to persons capable of moral agency. Thus, self-determination should serve to further what Michael Walzer has called the "communal autonomy" of the appropriate groups.[41]

But this is not a sufficient definition. The appropriate groups must be those for whom such autonomy can have a discernible effect on their well-being. The clearest case of this, I believe, is that of those peoples or substate regions that stand to lose from absorption within larger populations or countries. The reason is that the purpose of communal autonomy is best understood as redress for instances of what Allen Buchanan has called "discriminatory redistribution"—that is, the reallocation of goods, resources, or benefits of one group or region to those of another by a sovereign state ruling over both of them.[42]

What self-determination in general is designed to ensure is that the conditions for self-development are, as much as possible, in the hands of people themselves. Taking these conditions away from people is unjust. On this account, the principle of self-determination would be legitimately invoked in those cases in which problems of redistribution cannot be addressed by simply appealing to human rights or democratic entitlements.

It is appropriate, I believe, to characterize such cases as instances of regional self-determination since they necessarily involve locally specific uses of natural and human resources for the production of goods and the satisfaction of needs. Two types of cases in which the regional principle would apply are those of indigenous peoples who are trying to preserve a distinctive way of life and those of localities that are attempting to be or have been self-sufficient (i.e., ecologically sustainable). In both cases, it is the redistribution of natural resources or material wealth (through expropriation or taxation) from one population or area to another that is unjust or discriminatory and that would therefore provide grounds for a claim of self-determination.

Thus, a regional principle of self-determination might be the following: *if a group of persons living within a well-defined region of a country and pursuing a distinctive way of life is systematically disadvantaged by an entrenched and continuing pattern of discrimination in the allocation of goods and resources that prejudicially affects their ability to pursue their own way of life, that group has a right to redress through assertion of a principle of self-determination in the allocation and management of its own goods and resources.*

The warrant for this principle is that neither the concepts of human rights nor democratic self-government adequately address the problems of what have been called "internal colonialism" or "regional exploitation." The regional principle is designed to do this. It is important to note here that it would not necessarily mandate statehood—this would be a contingent matter, dependent on the possibility of obtaining some substantive autonomy within existing states. Rather, the regional principle is designed to serve as a conceptual alternative to that of national self-determination to get us to think differently about the enabling conditions of our cultural identities—conditions that are not reducible primarily to traditional ethnic or kinship affiliations but rather are more dependent on the actual places in which we live and the distinctive ways of life that dwelling in these places produces.[43]

Two kinds of cases may help to clarify what is meant by discriminatory redistribution in its different manifestations. First, take the case of indigenous peoples such as American Indian peoples (either in the United States and Canada or in Latin America), or minorities within large states in Asia, Europe, or Africa (such as the Tibetans in China). The mistreatment (to say the least) of American Indian peoples by European immigrants from the nineteenth century (up to our own time in many places) provides a prima facie reason for claiming self-determination within autonomous regions. This has, in fact, been the basis of attempts to redress the extreme disenfranchisement of American Indians in the United States and, especially, in Canada. In the case of the Tibetans (and, by extension, of other minorities), the efforts by China first to annex Tibet fully in the 1950s and, more recently, to eradicate the material and spiritual culture of the Tibetan people suggests that their case is one of what has been called indigenous rights—the claim of indigenous peoples to self-determination when faced with threats to their way of life. The regional principle is a way of giving reasons for such a claim not in terms of cultural identities but in terms of the preservation of different regional ways of life. Thus, when indigenous peoples such as the American Indians or the Tibetans assert a right of self-determination, it ought to be grounded on the existence of a threat to a distinctive way of life, rather than on the supposed right of culturally distinct nations to states. In fact, such indigenous peoples have often shown themselves to be primarily interested, not in statehood—as ought to be the case if they based their claims on the nationalist principle—but in some form of regional autonomy that does not directly challenge the sovereignty of existing states in which they reside. This may be the result not only of a pragmatic accommodation to political realities but also of a more subtle understanding of the limitations of a nationalistic, state-oriented view of self-determination than that found in other so-called national liberation movements.

A second kind of case is that of regions of a country subject to economic exploitation that disrupts the ability of such regions to sustain a way of life distinct from that of the rest of the country. Usually such discriminatory redistribution occurs through excessive taxation, but it may also occur through tariffs that affect production of goods in particular regions, changes in land tenure that grant property rights to outside persons or corporations, or the imposition of restrictions on forms of economic production such as farming or fishing. Such measures have threatened the livelihood and way of life of peoples in many regions of the world; examples could be drawn from the Maritime provinces of Canada, the Amazon region of Brazil, and the Siberian region of Russia, among others. In all such cases, self-determination is at issue because the redistribution of resources unfairly reallocates material wealth and opportunities—unfairly in the sense that they adversely affect the ability of peoples to live independent, self-sustaining lives based on particular regional environments.

What both cases of internal colonialism and regional exploitation thus present us with are examples of the lack of regional self-determination for peoples with ways of life that diverge from those politically dominant within larger countries. This is neither a problem subsumable within a nationalistic framework, since the idea of national culture is not adequately descriptive of differences between local and regional ecologies or one that a democratic principle can address, since it may actually be the decisions of democratic majorities within particular countries that lead to the problem in the first place.

CONCLUSION

The analysis of these cases should lead us to conclude, I would argue, that a concept of self-determination, when properly understood as a right of ecologically distinct regions, addresses certain problems of injustice and oppression otherwise missed by current moral and political theory. One could, however, also argue that by reconstituting the idea of self-determination in these terms, it is no longer suited to addressing the issues of cultural oppression and/or identity that the nationalist principle was designed to solve.

How, then, can problems of cultural discrimination be addressed, if not in terms of an ethical principle of collective self-determination, nationalist or otherwise? First, it must be remembered that the argument presented here was designed to show that there is no general right of national self-determination—that is, no right absent specific instances of national oppression or discrimination. But what about such instances? I would argue that they should be regarded as violations of existing human rights—as in the case of the right to a cultural nationality that is already recognized in international law. In other words, where national cultures are suppressed or persecuted, the appropriate means of redress are just those applicable to any other cases of human rights violations. No separate principle of national self-determination is warranted.

There is, however, still the issue of whether, in such cases of severe national oppression, the secession of the national group to create a new state of their own is ever warranted. Nothing stated here would necessarily preclude such a recourse, as long as it was understood that it involved asserting a principle of human rights, and not of national rights. But such a case, in which a group secedes from a state because of severe persecution, is not in substance different from other cases in which groups suffering human rights violations might claim just cause for secession. Thus, if such a claim is warranted in cases of genocide—the attempted extermination of a group—it could be warranted in cases of so-called cultural genocide—that is, the forcible suppression of a group's cultural practices. Of course, the potential costs of secession would have to be weighed against the benefits of free cultural expression—a weighing that would be noticeably easier in cases of simply survival in the face of physical attack.[44]

Finally, I want to take note of a potential problem with using the idea of discriminatory redistribution to define self-determination. As Buchanan notes, using the concept of discriminatory redistribution as a means of distinguishing legitimate from illegitimate claims to self-determination seems to require prior agreement about what constitutes a just distribution of resources. Without this, no consensus, philosophical, legal, or political, could be expected about when discriminatory redistribution is occurring.

But, as Buchanan maintains, it may not be necessary to reach agreement about a philosophical concept of justice before agreement could obtain concerning cases. What is required is a midrange, or substantive, conception that would indicate when discriminatory redistribution is occurring. As he notes, a historical example of this—namely, colonialism—did provide a basis for both philosophical and legal agreement about the necessity of redress (and this occurred without agreement on how to characterize the conception of justice or rights underlying condemnations of colonialism). Yet Buchanan is somewhat at a loss as to what such a midrange concept of justice might be in the postcolonial world.

I would argue that this is where reformulating self-determination—and discriminatory redistribution—in ecoregional terms lends itself to providing just such a midrange concept of distributive justice. In discussions of the environmental impact of economic development policies over the last twenty years, a new international consensus has emerged that rejects the old concepts of growth and modernization that were used to measure development. Instead, a new concept of sustainability has come into play as a means of gauging when development policies are appropriate for regions and ecosystems and when they are not. If development policies are unsustainable in terms of a region's natural resources and social structures, then they can be deemed unjust. So discriminatory redistribution, when applied to ecological regions (rather than social groups of all kinds), occurs when unsustainable development policies, including schemes of land tenure and resource allocation, are imposed.

Of course, the concept of sustainability has been the subject of much debate (as was that of colonialism) in terms of what it actually means, how to measure it, and whether it is compatible with development policies of various kinds. Views of these matters range from those that advocate "sustainable growth" to those that argue for the fundamental incompatibility of sustainability with development of any kind.[45] But such a debate also occurred about how to define colonialism—and it did not prevent the international community and most political philosophers from characterizing it as unjust.

An additional objection to the espousal of a regional principle of self-determination might be that such a principle would give encouragement to the fragmentation of political communities, much as has the nationalist principle. Regional self-determination might, on this account, undermine the bonds of solidarity that already obtain, in however weakened a form, within existing states and countries, as regional loyalties become more paramount. Such a development might already be seen in such countries as Britain and Spain, where regional loyalties have become more pronounced in recent years.

Such a criticism, however, is misplaced in two ways. First, the elimination of discriminatory redistribution does not, as does the nationalist principle, necessar-

ily place value or priority on statehood. Rather, it provides a justification for re-
dressing problems of inappropriate distributions of wealth and resources within
countries, without including any argument for regions obtaining their own states.
Secession would only become an option in cases in which there is no recognition
of, or willingness to redress, discriminatory redistribution. In that case, there
would be just cause for fragmenting a state in which some members act to prevent the attainment of a sustainable livelihood for others. In addition, it must be
emphasized that the weakening of state sovereignties in many cases might benefit the peoples living within them in terms of their ability to sustain distinctive
and ecologically sound ways of life.

Second, the criticism of fragmentation entails a misunderstanding of the nature
of ecoregionalism. Such a conception does not hold that no ties of obligation may
obtain between inhabitants of different regions—only that such ties must not
make impossible a sustainable way of life within regions. In fact, the focus on
ecological sustainability contains within it a universalist principle applicable potentially to all regions of the world. It may be seen to imply universal respect—
and even aid for—all peoples who wish to live within the ecological limits of
their respective environments. Furthermore, fragmentation of states would not
necessarily result from a focus on ecoregions. Many states—especially smaller
ones—exist within ecological regions, rather than being divided between them.
Other states might very well need to combine or federate in some way to cooperate for sustainable development.[46]

Once it is understood that the meaning of self-determination is not exhausted
by its use for democratic entitlements, nor is it generally applicable to national
groups seeking statehood, the idea can serve to highlight the importance of particularity, locality, and community as vital and enduring needs. Thought of in this
way, self-determination does not represent the attainment of the illusory community of the nation-state but a new type of autonomy that can protect different ways
of life and forms of ecological sustainability.

NOTES

1. For a discussion of these three phases of interest in the idea of self-determination,
see Rupert Emerson, "Self-Determination," *American Journal of International Law* 65
(1971): 459–75.

2. Jürgen Habermas, "Citizenship and National Identity: Some Reflections on the Future of Europe," *Praxis International* 12, no. 1 (April 1992): 1–18.

3. Wentworth Ofuatey-Kodjoe, *The Principle of Self-Determination in International
Law* (New York: Nellen, 1977), 150.

4. See Elie Kedourie, *Nationalism*, 4th ed. (Oxford: Blackwell, 1993) and, for exam-
ple, Gebre Hiwet Tesfagiorgis, "Self-Determination: Its Evolution and Practice by the
United Nations and Its Application to the Case of Eritrea," *Wisconsin International Law
Journal* 6 (1987).

5. Antonio Cassese, "The Self-Determination of Peoples," in *The International Bill of Rights: The Covenant on Civil and Political Rights*, ed. Louis Henkin (New York: Columbia University Press, 1981).

6. Ofuatey-Kodjoe, *Self-Determination in International Law*, 25.

7. See, for example, Charles Beitz, *Political Theory and International Relations* (Princeton, N.J.: Princeton University Press, 1979), and Thomas Pogge, *Realizing Rawls* (Ithaca, N.Y.: Cornell University Press, 1989).

8. However, to some extent, the apartheid regime was regarded as a special case in international law; see Emerson, "Self-Determination," 468.

9. On the Palestinian case in international law, see W. Thomas Mallison and Sally V. Mallison, *An International Law Analysis of the Major United Nations Resolutions Concerning the Palestine Question* (New York: United Nations, 1979), and Heather Wilson, *International Law and the Use of Force by National Liberation Movements* (Oxford: Clarendon, 1988).

10. This chapter is not primarily concerned with the idea that a principle of self-determination for political groups can be based on purely democratic grounds. This idea has received its most detailed exposition and defense from Harry Beran, particularly in his book *The Consent Theory of Political Obligation* (London: Croom Helm, 1987). It has also more recently been expressed by philosophers in the journals, see Daniel Philpott, "In Defense of Self-Determination," *Ethics* 105 (Jan. 1995): 352–85, and Kit Wellman, "A Defense of Secession and Self-Determination," 24, 2 (Spr. 1995): 142–71, *Philosophy and Public Affairs*. For a detailed critique of this idea, see chapter 3 of my Ph.D. dissertation, *A Critique of National Self-Determination* (City University of New York, 1995), entitled "Democracy, Consent, and Self-Determination." This critique can be summarized by stating that democratic consent cannot be used to determine membership in political communities, since the relevant population that would consent or dissent must always be stipulated prior to the operation of any democratic consensual procedure.

11. Some sources of the ethical justification of national self-determination are Charles Taylor, "Why Do Nations Have to Become States?" in *Philosophers Look at Canadian Confederation*, ed. Stanley G. French (Montreal: Canadian Philosophical Association, 1979); Joseph Raz, *The Morality of Freedom* (Oxford: Clarendon, 1986); Avishai Margalit and Joseph Raz, "National Self-Determination," *Journal of Philosophy* 87 (September 1990): 439–61; Yael Tamir, *Liberal Nationalism* (Princeton, N.J.: Princeton University Press, 1993); and Will Kymlicka, *Multicultural Citizenship: A Liberal Theory of Minority Rights* (Oxford: Clarendon, 1995).

12. Margalit and Raz, "National Self-Determination," 449.

13. Margalit and Raz, "National Self-Determination," 456–57.

14. Margalit and Raz, "National Self-Determination," 443–46.

15. Margalit and Raz, "National Self-Determination," 449.

16. See Kedourie, *Nationalism*, for discussion of the Kantian foundations of the concept of political self-determination.

17. Margalit and Raz, "National Self-Determination," 454.

18. Margalit and Raz, "National Self-Determination," 459. This does not mean that a claim of self-determination can never be wrongly asserted, but that the "right reason" is that an encompassing group is autonomously deciding its own political identity. If this reason is present, the national group then has the "right to decide." Furthermore, such a right is essential given the absence of other mechanisms for reliably determining a national

group's interests. It is the "absence of effective enforcement machinery in the international arena" that entails that decisions about political identity be left in the hands of groups themselves (Margalit and Raz, "National Self-Determination," 461).

19. Robert Musil, "'Nation' as Ideal and Reality," in *Precision and Soul: Essays and Addresses*, trans. Burton Pike and David S. Luft (Chicago: University of Chicago Press, 1990).

20. For the relation between the Hegelian idea of recognition and the contemporary concept of self-determination, see Charles Taylor, "The Politics of Recognition," in *Multiculturalism and "The Politics of Recognition,"* ed. Taylor et al. (Princeton, N.J.: Princeton University Press, 1992).

21. Taylor, "Politics of Recognition," 60–61.

22. Kymlicka, *Multicultural Citizenship*, 80.

23. On nationalist uses of the concept of cultural enjoyment, see Slavoj Zizek, "Eastern Europe's Republics of Gilead," *New Left Review* 183 (September–October 1990): 50–62, and *Tarrying with the Negative: Kant, Hegel, and the Critique of Ideology* (Durham, N.C.: Duke University Press, 1993).

24. Tamir, *Liberal Nationalism*, 85.

25. The concept of "symbolic citizenship," introduced by Avishai Margalit in his book *The Decent Society*, trans. Naomi Goldblum (Cambridge, Mass.: Harvard University Press, 1996), captures some aspects of this relation between culture and the state (though not in the way that Margalit here intends).

26. On the connection between nation-states and official cultures, see Anthony Giddens, *The Nation-State and Violence*, vol. 2 of *A Contemporary Critique of Historical Materialism* (Berkeley: University of California Press, 1987).

27. Yael Tamir, "The Right to National Self-Determination," *Social Research* 58, no. 3 (Fall 1991): 577.

28. Iris Young, *Justice and the Politics of Difference* (Princeton, N.J.: Princeton University Press, 1990), 157.

29. As Ross Poole has pointed out in his book *Morality and Modernity* (London: Routledge, 1991, 98–99), they are only one form that cultures have taken, often by obliterating other local or transnational forms.

30. It is important to note that nationalists do usually assume, rather than argue for, such a view of identity. For instance, Tamir writes, "National rights can only be consistently justified on universal grounds by referring to the value individuals find in the existence of nations, and by *assuming* that human beings care as much about the national environment in which they implement their life-plans as about the specific content of these plans" (*Liberal Nationalism*, 83, italics added) But this is exactly what needs to be demonstrated, not just assumed (and, in fact, there is much evidence to the contrary).

31. Dov Ronen, *The Quest for Self-Determination* (New Haven, Conn.: Yale University Press, 1979), 53.

32. Ronen, *Quest for Self-Determination*, 52.

33. Ronen, *Quest for Self-Determination*, 61.

34. Tamir, "Right to National Self-Determination," 585.

35. This point is made very tellingly by William McNeill in his book *Polyethnicity and National Unity in World History* (Toronto: University of Toronto Press, 1986).

36. As Max Horkheimer and Theodor Adorno write in *Dialectic of Enlightenment*, trans. John Cumming (New York: Continuum, 1982; originally published, 1944), "The

idolization of the cheap involves making the average the heroic. . . . It is all a parody of the never-never land, just as the national society is a parody of the human society" (156).

37. Karl Marx, "On the Jewish Question," in *The Marx–Engels Reader*, 2d ed., ed. Robert Tucker (New York: Norton, 1978), 34.

38. Margalit and Raz, "National Self-Determination," 450–51.

39. Margalit and Raz, "National Self-Determination," 450–51.

40. Lea Brilmayer, "Groups, Histories, and International Law," *Cornell International Law Journal* 25, no. 3 (1992 symposium): 559.

41. For the concept of communal autonomy, see Michael Walzer, *Just and Unjust Wars: A Moral Argument with Historical Illustrations* (New York: Basic Books, 1977). It must be said that, though I agree in general terms with Walzer's notion of communal autonomy, I disagree with the communitarian direction in which Walzer, and others such as David Miller, have taken this idea. For a critique of this communitarian position, see my article "The Nation-State as a Political Community: A Critique of the Communitarian Argument for National Self-Determination," in *Rethinking Nationalism*, ed. Jocelyne Couture, Kai Nielsen, and Michel Seymour (Supplementary Volume 22 of the *Canadian Journal of Philosophy* [1998]): 311–43. In general, the communitarian position poses three problems: an impoverished conception of political community (based on a nationalistic view of the state), the threat to any system of peaceful accommodation between communities posed by a justification of nationalistic aspirations, and the inadequacy of nation-states for achieving real communal self-determination. There are the additional problems of an inadequate conception of culture (based on a primordialist view of national affinities) and the lack of means for determining legitimate claims to territory, on which assertions of the rights of national communities depend. These latter deficiencies point to the difference between a nationalistic understanding of community and the ecological perspective outlined here, which relies on a view of culture that emphasizes distinctive forms of political ecology, rather than beliefs about kinship ties or national character.

42. On the concept of "discriminatory redistribution," see Allen E. Buchanan, *Secession: The Morality of Political Divorce from Fort Sumter to Lithuania and Quebec* (Boulder, Colo.: Westview, 1991).

43. On this contrast, see Lewis Mumford, *The Culture of Cities* (New York: Harcourt Brace Jovanovich, 1938), 354.

44. For a thoughtful discussion of the considerations to be taken into account in such cases, see Buchanan, *Secession*.

45. See, for some discussion of these debates, M. R. Redclift, *Sustainable Development: Exploring the Contradictions* (London: Methuen, 1987), and Vandana Shiva, "Recovering the Meaning of Sustainability," in *The Environment in Question: Ethics and Global Issues*, ed. David Cooper and Joy Palmer (London: Routledge, 1992).

46. This seems to be the case, for instance, in the Middle East, where the watershed of the Jordan River encompasses all or part of Israel (including the occupied territories), Jordan, and Syria. It also might be the case in other large watersheds, such as those of the Danube, Nile, or Congo Rivers, as well as in regions such as island archipelagos (the Caribbean) or those around inland seas (e.g., the Aral, Caspian, or Black Seas). Other geographic examples of transnational regions could no doubt be found.

2

✛

Peoples, Nations,
and the Unity of Societies

CHRISTOPHER W. MORRIS

What makes a society *one*? A common view in Enlightenment cultures such as those of the United States or France is that a society is one because its people are one. Peoples, in this view, are prior to states. In the American case, "We the People" are held to have constituted the state, and in the French tradition sovereignty is ascribed to *la nation* or *le peuple*. 'The people' in this sense (with the definite article) is to be distinguished from 'a people' or 'peoples' (with the indefinite article). The latter are collections whose unity is primarily social, as opposed to political, much like nations and ethnic groups. The distinction is important for Enlightenment cultures with cosmopolitan self-conceptions. Understanding the unity of well-ordered societies to depend on social ties (e.g., nationality) would threaten their universalist pretensions.

Or so it is widely thought. Thomas Jefferson, the patron saint of the American version of this story, asserts that governments derive "their just powers from the consent of the governed" and that "it is the right of the people to alter or abolish" governments destructive of the proper ends of securing the rights of life, liberty, and the pursuit of happiness. He also asserts in the opening paragraph of the very same Declaration of Independence that "one people," when distinct from another, is entitled by the laws of nature to a "separate and equal station" (i.e., independence). A careful reading of the text makes apparent the distinction between a people and the people. Jefferson, it appears, does not subscribe to the view that the unity of well-ordered societies should not depend on the particular social relationships or ties of members. In fact, he thinks that distinct peoples are entitled to independence. The ignorance or neglect of his protonationalism may suggest that the contemporary self-image of cosmopolitan Enlightenment states is suspect. I shall suggest this as well as the thought that a commitment to certain universal rights of persons is compatible with understanding the unity of well-ordered societies to be based, at least in part, on particular social relations.

What makes a society *one*? What is, to ask the question in an old-fashioned manner, the principle of individuation of societies? We count the United States and France, for instance, as single societies in this sense. So it is natural to ask whether the principle of individuation is simply being a *political society*. Today virtually all political societies are *states*.[1] Is being a state what makes a society one, then? In this view, the United States and France are societies, as are Italy, Canada, and Belgium. Our enumeration of societies would correspond more or less to what political geographers offer us when they map the world, using different colors for different countries.

This answer is not, however, acceptable in the dominant American and French political traditions. In these traditions the people are held to institute the state. The U.S. Constitution attributes the constitutive power to the people in its famous opening words: "We the People of the United States . . . do ordain and establish this Constitution for the United States of America." The French *Déclaration des droits de l'homme et du citoyen*, enacted by the representatives of the French people in 1789, ascribes sovereign authority not to the monarch but to the nation: "Le principe de toute souveraineté réside essentiellement dans la nation" (Art. 3). The Constitution of the Fifth Republic (1958) reaffirms this principle of popular sovereignty: "La souveraineté nationale appartient au peuple, qui l'exercise par ses représentants et par la voie du référendum" (Art. 3). The people (or *la nation*) must be understood as prior to the state if they are to play this constituting role. So the individuating power of the state must be derivative from the prior unity of the people.[2]

The priority of the people underscores the *instrumentalist* conception of the state or government characteristic of these traditions. Government is understood to serve the interests of the governed.[3] The American Declaration of Independence agrees with the French *Déclaration* in asserting that government is instituted to secure the fundamental rights of men. Political institutions are means to an end and to be evaluated accordingly. As the rights of men[4] figure prominently among the cited ends of government, these political traditions tend to *consensualism*: the just powers of governments derive "from the consent of the governed." Men have certain inalienable or natural rights, including the right to liberty.[5] Only consent, it may be thought, could legitimate government.

We might think that the people are the principle of individuation of societies: one people, one society. What makes the people one? The answer offered by Nazi partisans of *Ein Volk, ein Staat, ein Führer* is a people made one by ties of history and blood. It is thought, however, that this cannot be the sort of unity consistent with the universal principles of right of the American and French traditions. Let us distinguish more precisely '*the* people' from '*a* people'. 'The People' (hereafter with a capital P), in its modern sense, is a term that originally designated the members of the nonaristocratic (and nonclerical) classes of society. The radical idea of the French Revolution was that these classes (or their representatives) had the right to rule, contra the claim of all of the European aristocracies.[6] Gradually 'the People' comes to be more inclusive, covering at least all members of the polity and sometimes all subject to its governance (including, e.g., nonmember residents). The old connotations of the term remain—"he is a man of the people"—but generally, it is now to be understood in these contexts to include almost every inhabitant of a state. This notion of the People echoes classical Roman ideas, as does its associated notion of citizenship. 'A people', by contrast, designates a collective entity whose unity is social and not primarily political. The notion of a people, then, is similar to that of a nation or ethnic group; it is of a group of humans united by ties of history, culture, or "blood."[7]

The individuation of Peoples (with the definite article) is considerably more problematic than has been noticed. What is surprising perhaps is the casualness with which political thinkers have assumed that Peoples are readily identifiable. Certainly, prior to modern states, it is hard to identify Peoples in our general or inclusive sense. With the advent of the state, the People becomes identified with the bulk of its subjects or residents. But we are not supposed to believe that states determine who constitutes Peoples. For it is "We the People" who are meant to be constituting the state in the first place! If states are prior, then their constitution by the People becomes impossible.[8]

If the People are constituted as such prior to the state, then their unity must be prior and independent. How might this be? In keeping with the consensualism of the American and French political traditions, it might be thought that Peoples are constituted voluntarily through consent. A People is made one, in this view, by the consent of its members. Consent figures prominently in the social contract theories of the seventeenth and eighteenth centuries. Jean-Jacques Rousseau asks about "l'acte par lequel un peuple est un peuple." He famously seeks the unity of a people in a social pact involving the total alienation of each person to the community under the direction of the general will; "cet acte d'association produit un corps moral et collectif composé d'autant de membres que l'assemblé a de voix, lequel reçoit de ce même acte son unité, son moi commun, sa vie et sa volonté."[9] Rousseau's account is distinctively populist, whereas Thomas Hobbes's otherwise similar account (of "Sovereignty by Institution") is statist. For the latter, individuals "conferre all their power and strength upon one Man, or upon one Assembly of men, that may reduce all their Wills, by a plurality of voices, unto one Will. . . . This is more than Consent, or Concord; it is a real Unitie of them all, in one and the same Person. . . . This done, the Multitude so united in one Person, is called a Common-wealth."[10]

Talk of consent in Hobbes's and Rousseau's works, however, is misleading since the "consent" in question seems to be hypothetical rather than actual. Consent is an act of the will and, to be genuine, must be actual (explicit or tacit).[11] John Locke, by contrast, is a genuine consensualist:

> Men being, as has been said, by Nature, all free, equal and independent, no one can be put out of this Estate, and subjected to the Political Power of another, without his own *Consent*. The only way whereby any one divests himself of his Natural Liberty, and *puts on the bonds of Civil Society* is by agreeing with other Men to joyn and unite into a Community. . . . When any number of Men have so *consented to make one Community* or Government, they are thereby presently incorporated and make *one Body Politick*.[12]

Without exploring some of the interpretative and theoretical issues regarding Locke's account, we can acknowledge the possibility of explaining the unity of some Peoples by their constituent members' actual—explicit or tacit—consent.[13] However, the unity of none of the Peoples we have in mind—the French, the American, the Italian, the Japanese—could be so explained. The individuals in questions cannot plausibly all be said to have consented in the requisite manner.[14]

The hypothetical consent invoked by Hobbes and Rousseau may seem to fare better in terms of underpinning the unity of Peoples. But one needs to ask why a particular set of persons—say, all French people or all Americans—are thought to have consented hypothetically. It may well be plausible to think that all such persons would have agreed to something like the present political institutions and arrangements; let us grant the point. But this does not instruct as to why we select *this* particular set of people for our investigation about hypothetical consent. Why investigate what all Americans would agree to unless we thought that the set of living Americans possessed some prior unity? Why not all persons on the Continent or all living west of the Rockies or the Mississippi? Presumably hypothetical consent theorists have an independent way of individuating Peoples. In *A Theory of Justice*, John Rawls restricts his attentions to a society "conceived for the time being as a closed system isolated from other societies," and he assumes that "the boundaries of these schemes are given by the notion of a self-contained national community."[15] Hypothetical consent as a justificatory device in political theory seems to presuppose an independent determination of the relevant set of individuals.[16] If this is right, hypothetical consent will be of little use in establishing the unity of the People.

We could simply identify the People with "the governed." But this is problematic for the same reason: the identity of the relevant set of governed persons is not prior to or independent of the state in question. There are other problems with this suggestion. The governed consist of subjects and citizens, the latter being a proper subset of the former. The notion of "a subject" here is not, of course, the classical one of someone who is *subjugated* to another; a subject in this formal sense is merely someone *subject to* the laws of a state or polity. Foreigners, whether residing or just passing through, are subjects but not citizens. Normally, one might identify the People with the set of full members—that is, citizens. But this is not always plausible, for instance, prior to "universal suffrage." In the case of states or empires with colonies or governing "subjected peoples," many subjects would not have the status of membership (e.g., many Palestinians in Israeli-occupied territories). In some other states, there may be many more nonmember residents than citizens (e.g., Kuwait, Monaco).[17]

Political theorists often appear to assume that individuating Peoples or societies is not problematic. Rawls is typical in assuming that societies are easily individuated. However, in most cases, in which the geographic setting is not saliently one and distinct—as, for instance, with an island—or in which the individuals do not evidently constitute a single people or nation, the attribution of unity to "the society" seems question begging.[18] Our identification of societies seem to depend on that of states. However genuine the unity that we attribute to societies, it seems to be a consequence of their form of political organization—namely, the state.

A perspicuous and plausible account of the concept of a society has been offered by David Copp. He argues that societies are to be understood in terms of a number of key characteristics. They are multigenerational and extended in time. Membership in them is not, at least initially, a matter of choice. Members interact among themselves in a number of ways, especially in activities related to securing the materials necessities of life, and these interactions are governed by a system of rules accepted, at least implicitly, by members. And "a society provides the framework for its members' lives, embracing the bulk of their friends and socially most important acquaintances." Copp summarizes his account thus: "Roughly, a society is a multigenerational, temporally extended population of persons, embracing a relatively closed network of relationships of friendship, affection, kinship, and cooperation in reproduction, and limited by the widest boundary of a distinctive system of instrumental interaction."[19] The account allows for societies to be conflicted: "Societies are not ideal communities; they are not necessarily united by a common aim, interest, or moral ideal." In his view, "societies are unified, not by means of a sense of commonality or an absence of conflict, but by a unity forged from an overlapping network of social relationships, including instrumental interaction governed by salient standards."[20]

It is a virtue of Copp's account that societies can overlap and be nested one within another. This agrees with our commonsense judgments (e.g., Catalonia is part of Spain; Basque society overlaps with France and Spain). But it is not clear, for instance, that Europe is a society, as Copp believes, or that "the population of the European Community also constitutes a society."[21] The concern here is not over the concept of a society but over the interactions among Europeans that are supposed to make them members of a European society. The case of medieval Europe is more interesting. I would be skeptical, for instance, about the existence of a medieval European society, and I certainly think there were no medieval societies corresponding to the political societies we now take to make up Europe. In Copp's account, being a society (rightly) is a matter of degree. But the issues raised by medieval Europe is not that. Rather, the patterns of interaction in medieval Europe were not, I believe, of the right kind to constitute societies corresponding, even roughly, to the French, English, Italian, or Swiss societies of today. The case of medieval Europe is important, for the absence of counterparts to modern European countries suggests that the explanation for the unity of these societies lies, in virtually all cases, with the particular form of political organization assumed by virtually all contemporary political societies—namely, the state. However plausible as an analysis of our concept of society, Copp's account offers no independent explanation of the unity of contemporary political societies. As he says elsewhere, "Many societies are to some extent the product of the division of the world into states, and in virtually every case where a state governs a population, that population constitutes a society."[22] The patterns of interaction that determine the identity or boundaries of our societies typically are those mandated or facilitated by states.

I said earlier that Enlightenment political cultures with cosmopolitan self-conceptions such as France or the United States rebel against understanding social unity as based on social ties such as nationality or ethnic identity. In our political traditions, the People are not to be understood as a people. Thus, we cannot try to individuate Peoples by identifying them with peoples (with the indefinite article). To do so would be inconsistent with our cosmopolitan traditions. Or would it?

Consider the founding document of the American political tradition, the Declaration of Independence of 1776. The famous second paragraph, known by heart by most Americans, ascribes certain rights to men (presumably to all humans): "We hold these truths to be self-evident: that all men are created equal; that they are endowed by their Creator with certain inalienable rights; that among these are life, liberty, and the pursuit of happiness; that to secure these rights, governments are instituted among men, deriving their just powers from the consent of the governed." This ascription of individual rights is central to the self-understanding of Americans and constitutive of the moral individualism of our political culture. It is not clear, however, that this self-image is consistent with Jefferson's text. The Declaration continues: "[W]henever any form of government becomes destructive of these ends, it is the right of *the people* to alter or abolish it, and to institute new government, laying its foundation on such principles, and organizing its powers in such form, as to them shall seem most likely to effect their safety and happiness" (emphasis added). The right to alter or abolish unjust or tyrannical government, the fourth right explicitly mentioned in the Declaration, is ascribed to "the people." Unlike the other rights, it seems to be a collective right, presumably like the implicit right of "We the People" in the Constitution of 1789, the founding document of the American state.

It is the opening paragraph of the Declaration that is the most interesting for our purposes. I cite it in full: "When, in the course of human events, it becomes necessary for *one people* to dissolve the political bands which have connected them with another, and to assume among the powers of the earth the separate and equal station to which the laws of nature and of nature's God entitle them, a decent respect to the opinions of mankind requires that they should declare the causes which impel them to the separation" (emphasis added). What is remarkable (and rarely noticed) in this paragraph is the ascription of certain entitlements to single peoples. The famous opening paragraph asserts that a people, such as the one British Americans have become, are compelled "to assume among the powers of the earth the separate & equal station to which the laws of nature . . . entitle them." Single peoples have entitlements by natural law. Not only are these entitlements collective, but they are ascribed to "one people." Invoking the distinction I drew between the People and a people, it seems reasonable to interpret the collective right to alter or abolish unjust government to the first; the right to rebel is the collective right of the People or at least the governed. But the right to assume a separate and equal station among the powers of the Earth (i.e., independent states) is an entitlement of peoples (with the indefinite article).

Lest we be thought to be leaping to conclusions let us look at other passages in Jefferson's Declaration.[23] In a long paragraph, famously deleted by Congress, Jefferson complains about King George's imposition of the "execrable commerce" in slaves: "[He has waged cruel war against human nature itself, violating its most sacred rights of life and liberty in the persons of *a distant people* who never offended him, captivating and carrying them into slavery in another hemisphere, or to incur miserable death in their transportation hither]" (emphasis added). Lamenting our separation from the people of Great Britain, Jefferson notes that "we have appealed to their native justice and magnanimity and we have conjured them by the ties of *our common kindred* to disavow these usurpations which would inevitably interrupt our connection and correspondence. They too have been deaf to the voice of justice and of *consanguinity*" (emphasis added). Having complained in an earlier passage of the king's "transporting large armies of *foreign* mercenaries to complete the works of death, desolation and tyranny already begun," Jefferson continues his lament to "our British *brethren*": "[At this very time too, they are permitting their chief magistrate to send over not only soldiers of *our common blood*, but *Scotch and foreign* mercenaries to invade and destroy us. These facts have given the last stab to agonizing affection, and manly spirit bids us to renounce forever these unfeeling *brethren*. . . . We might have been *a free and a great people* together]" (emphases added).

I quote at length from the Declaration, especially passages excised from Jefferson's original draft, as evidence of his use of the notion of peoples (with the indefinite article) as a socially determined set of individuals. However unaware of this Jefferson himself may have been, both notions of people are evident in his Declaration. We might dispute his particular characterization or individuation of our British brethren—some of his fellows might have bristled at the complaint against the king sending over "not only soldiers of our common blood, but Scotch & foreign mercenaries." But the oft-used language of brotherhood and consanguinity suggest social ties of a nationalist or ethnic kind.

Jefferson's ascription of the rights of life and liberty to black Africans, "a distant people," also suggests a genuine universalism. The position we might attribute to him would assign the rights to life, liberty, and the pursuit of happiness to individuals, the right to rebel to the People, and the entitlements to statehood (a separate and equal station) to single peoples. I do not, however, wish to engage in scholarly disputes about the interpretation of Jefferson's thought. I want instead to make a limited number of claims. It is striking how rarely noticed are these ethnonationalist sentiments in our founding document. There is a certain mystification in the self-image of Enlightenment political cultures like ours.[24]

Additionally, whatever is decided about the best interpretation of Jefferson's thought, we can see how it might be possible to combine a commitment to (certain) universal rights of persons with understanding the unity of societies to be based, at least in part, on particular social relations.[25] The antagonism to nationalism characteristic of the American and French political traditions is not only lacking in self-awareness but possibly unnecessary.

One might also try to individuate Peoples by identifying them with peoples; the People, thus, is constituted by a people. But this too is unpromising. There are some plausible accounts of the claims of peoples or national groups to independence. However, they tend to impose a number of conditions and constraints on the rights of peoples (or "encompassing groups"), and these make it impossible to generalize the identification of peoples and Peoples.[26] In the American context, we might just note that the identification of the People with the "one people" referred to in Jefferson's Declaration would exclude Africans, native peoples, and some European immigrants from citizenship.[27]

It may well be that the unity of our societies is not, for the most part, prior to and independent of their characteristic form of political organization—namely, the state. And some part of that unity may often be social in its origins–for instance, national. Neither of these facts need threaten our endorsement of universal principles of right or our ascription of fundamental rights to individuals, or so I have suggested. The unity of our societies may be thought to be somewhat contingent and fragile as a consequence. Perhaps this is so: but rather than something to be lamented, we might welcome this discovery. For it is not clear that the value of social unity always stands with certain universal elements of justice.[28]

NOTES

1. The exceptions for the most part are pseudostates or the remnants of other kinds of premodern political societies—for instance, the Vatican and the Principality of Monaco.

See Christopher W. Morris, *An Essay on the Modern State* (Cambridge: Cambridge University Press, 1998), especially chap. 2.

2. Bernard Yack notes that

> liberal democratic culture *itself* inspires people to think of themselves as members of prepolitical communities. This is especially true of the rhetoric of popular sovereignty. Popular sovereignty arguments encourage modern citizens to think of themselves as organized into communities that are logically and historically prior to the communities created by their shared political institutions. . . . The doctrine of popular sovereignty insists that behind every state stands a people, a community of individuals that makes use of the state as a means of self-government and thus has the right to establish the limits of its power.

Bernard Yack, "The Myth of the Civic Nation," *Critical Review* 10, no. 2 (Spring 1996): 200–201. See also my "Popular Sovereignty, the Very Idea," *Social Philosophy & Policy* 17, no. 1 (Winter 2000): 1–26.

3. This is what Joseph Raz calls "the service conception of the function of authorities, that is, the view that their role and primary normal function is to serve the governed." *The Morality of Freedom* (Oxford: Clarendon, 1986), 56. See my *Essay on the Modern State*, 5–6.

4. I use the allegedly generic term *man* in talking of the rights of men—*les droits de l'homme*—without, of course, wishing to endorse the consequently ambiguous political status of women.

5. See the second paragraph of the Declaration of Independence and Article 2 of the *Déclaration*.

6. "Les hommes naissent et demeurent libre et égaux en droits. Les distinctions sociales ne peuvent être fondées que sur l'utilité commune" (Art. 1). See also Article 3 quoted earlier.

7. See my *Essay on the Modern State*, sect. 8.2.

8. If this is right, it is not possible both to ascribe sovereignty to "We the People" and to say, as Akhil Amar says, that the American People are or were constituted by the state or the Constitution. See Amar, "Of Sovereignty and Federalism," *Yale Law Journal* 96, no. 7 (June 1987): 1463, n. 163 ("the most important thing that the Constitution constitutes is neither the national government, nor even the supreme law, but one sovereign national People, who may alter their government or supreme law at will."), and "The Consent of the Governed: Constitutional Amendment Outside Article V," *Columbia Law Review* 94 (March 1994): 489 ("the Constitution formed previously separate state peoples into one continental people—American!—by substituting a true [and self-described] Constitution for a true [and self-described] league").

9. Jean-Jacques Rousseau, *Du contract social*, Book I, chap. 6, in *Oeuvres complètes*, vol. III (Paris: Bibliothèque de la Pléiade, 1964), 359, 361.

10. Thomas Hobbes, *Leviathan*, ed. Richard Tuck (Cambridge: Cambridge University Press, 1991), chaps. 17, 120.

11. See Raz, *Morality of Freedom*, n. 81 ("Theories of hypothetical consent discuss not consent but cognitive agreement"); Morris, "The Relation of Self-Interest and Justice in Contractarian Ethics," *Social Philosophy & Policy* 5, no. 2 (Spring 1988): 121–22, and "A Contractarian Account of Moral Justification," in *Moral Knowledge? New Readings in Moral Epistemology*, ed. Walter Sinnott-Armstrong and Mark Timmons (New York: Oxford University Press, 1996), 219–20; Gerald Gaus, *Value and*

Justification (Cambridge: Cambridge University Press, 1990), 9, 328; and A. John Simmons, *On the Edge of Anarchy: Locke, Consent, and the Limits of Society* (Princeton, N.J.: Princeton University Press, 1993), 78–79 (hypothetical contract theory bases "our duties or obligations not on anyone's actual choices, but on whether our governments [states, laws] are sufficiently just, good, useful, or responsive to secure the hypothetical support of ideal choosers . . . the "contract" in hypothetical contractarianism is simply a device that permits us to analyze in a certain way quality of government").

In the same passages as quoted here, Hobbes speaks of "the Covenant of every man with every man, in such a manner, *as if* every man should say to every man" (emphasis added). "Sovereignty by Acquisition," Hobbes's second way of establishing a commonwealth or state, would not satisfy our conditions for genuine consent given that it is acquired by force.

12. John Locke, *Second Treatise of Government*, in *Two Treatises of Government*, ed. Peter Laslett (Cambridge: Cambridge University Press, 1988), chap. 8, para. 95.

13. For a perspicuous account of the relevant kinds of consent, see Simmons, *On the Edge of Anarchy: Locke, Consent, and the Limits of Society*, chap. 3.

14. Agreement on this point seems so widespread in the contemporary literature that defense is not needed. References may be found in Simmons's work cited earlier or in my *Essay on the Modern State*, especially sect. 6.4.

15. John Rawls, *A Theory of Justice* (Cambridge, Mass.: Harvard University Press, 1971), 8, 457.

16. Yack, "The Myth of the Civic Nation," 200.

> Social contract arguments serve to legitimate . . . different ways of ordering the social and political relationships within a predefined group of individuals. For these arguments assume that there is sufficient reason for individuals deliberating about justice and the social contract to pay attention to each other's proposals and decisions, rather than to those made by individuals outside of this group. Since the whole point of these theories is to determine the proper order within a given group of individuals, the assumption of a prepolitical community is safely tucked away in most of the debates about the meaning of liberal democratic principles.

17. Additionally, especially in an increasingly interdependent world, there are third parties, neither citizens nor subjects, whose lives are affected in important ways by states' decisions. Simply excluding them by fiat, by identifying the People with citizens or subjects, seems question begging.

18. Even with islands, attributing unity may be problematic (e.g., Ireland or England).

19. David Copp, *Morality, Normativity, and Society* (New York: Oxford University Press, 1995), chap. 7 (citations, 127).

20. Copp, *Morality, Normativity, and Society*, 139.

21. Copp, *Morality, Normativity, and Society*, 126, 139.

22. Copp, "The Idea of a Legitimate State," *Philosophy & Public Affairs* 28, no. 1 (Winter 1999): 37–38. Copp notes the existence of a French-speaking society in Quebec and a Cree society in northern Quebec as examples of societies that are "not dependent on their having states all to themselves." The examples are in fact compatible with my contention that our societies tend to be determined by states. The Cree, like other conquered peoples (and the Principality of Monaco mentioned earlier), are remnants of a world prior to states and exceptional as such. And where it used to flourish in Ontario, Manitoba, and elsewhere, French-speaking society now is confined to Que-

bec, a subunit of the federal Canadian state. Note, for instance, it is only the existence of the American and Canadian states that would have us think of European settlers living in nineteenth-century Maine or Minnesota as members of American society and similarly with their fellows across the border.

23. Citations of some of the passages deleted by Congress from Jefferson's original draft are in brackets and are from *The Portable Thomas Jefferson*, ed. Merrill D. Peterson (Harmondsworth, Middlesex: Penguin 1975), 236–41.

24. "[T]he idea of the civic nation, with its portrayal of community as a shared and rational choice of universally valid principles, is itself a cultural inheritance in nations like France and the United States. One aspect of distinctly French and American political ideologies is to portray their own cultural inheritance as a universally valid object of rational choice." Yack, "The Myth of the Civic Nation," 209, n. 3. An examination of similar mystifications in the French tradition might start with a critical examination of Dominique Schnapper, *La communauté des citoyens: sur l'idée moderne de nation* (Paris: Gallimard, 1994).

25. See, for instance, Yael Tamir, *Liberal Nationalism* (Princeton, N.J.: Princeton University Press, 1993), and Will Kymlicka, *Multicultural Citizenship* (Oxford: Clarendon, 1995).

26. See, in addition to the works cited in the previous note, Avishai Margalit and Joseph Raz, "National Self-Determination," *Journal of Philosophy* 87, no. 9 (September 1990): 439–61.

27. In addition to black Africans and "merciless Indian savages," Scotch and German persons, presumably, were alien and could not easily join the separate people Jefferson envisaged.

28. Some of the ways in which principles of sovereignty have been mistakenly thought to override certain considerations of justice are examined in my *Essay on the Modern State*, chaps. 7, 10, and "Popular Sovereignty, the Very Idea."

3

Could Canada Turn into Bosnia?

FRANK CUNNINGHAM

Shortly after the election in Quebec of the sovereigntist Parti Québecois (the PQ) and one year before that party's 1980 referendum aimed at taking the province out of the Canadian Confederation, the Canadian Philosophical Association convened a conference to address the country's constitutional crisis. The event took place in Montreal, bringing together philosophers from all regions of the country. Charles Taylor gave the keynote address, "Why Do Nations Have to Become States?" Roundtables were organized on national self-determination, constitutional options, and individual and collective rights. The PQ lost its 1980 referendum but held another one in 1995, which also failed but by less than one percentage point, with a majority of Francophones in the Province supporting it. Reelected in 1998, this party continues to pursue a sovereigntist politics. Hence, contributions to the conference as well as subsequent interventions by Canadian political philosophers addressing the themes the association put before itself are still relevant.[1]

Reviewing the collective efforts of the philosophers at that time, I find that deficiencies are not in the content of the contributions but in a certain timidity and a glaring absence. Care was taken to include philosophers from Quebec and all regions of the country outside it. Absent was any representation from Canada's Aboriginal communities. Nor, with the exception of a few parenthetical references, were there discussions of issues especially concerning Native peoples. I shall return to this absence at the end of the chapter, the bulk of which will address a topic the philosophers carefully skirted around—namely, the potential for violent conflict, on which, as will be seen shortly, the situation of Aboriginal peoples in the country has a direct bearing.

VIOLENCE

In focusing on violence I do not mean to suggest that I think it likely. However, in today's world Canadians would do well to avoid complacency, and there may be something to learn about how to minimize national conflict by looking at its limiting case. Political philosophy is well suited to this task. It is of its nature to identify the most extreme aspect of a subject matter, no matter how rare or improbable, and to try constructing theories that will accommodate it. Ethics or the philosophy of language would be too easy if they ignored lifeboat dilemmas or radical indeterminacy of translation. Another reason that political philosophy can address the possibility of violence is that this carries little danger of creating it. If foes of Quebec sovereignty (called "federalists" in current Canadian discourse) in the government or military leaders began publicly examining different violent scenarios, these could turn into self-fulfilling prophecies. But in Canada philosophy does not provoke such reactions, as few in the general public have thought of philosophers as politically efficacious enough to be threatening (though some have rightly feared the use or misuse of philosophical theories in the hands of those who *are* political effective).

Well, then, could Canada turn into Bosnia? To address this question, I shall first survey some recent philosophical or philosophically informed theories about the nature and causes of violent ethnonational conflict, such as those in the Near East, Ireland, South Asia, and Eastern Europe.[2] Dissatisfaction with such theories leads me to an alternate approach, which I shall apply to the Canadian case, drawing upon recent philosophical writings about nations and nationalism.

Main approaches to the question of ethnic violence at levels of philosophical abstraction have appealed to putative features of human nature. Aside from theological accounts in terms of original human depravity, the main theories I shall survey are those of the sociobiologists, the cultural theory of René Girard, and Russell Hardin's deployment of rational choice theory. I confess to being antecedently skeptical of these theories, due to suspicion of any political approach rooted in a conception of human nature, which seem to me to have a question-begging, "dormative powers"–like character about them. Though I shall note some useful things to be learned from each of the approaches, I think that suspicion of their adequacy as full-blown analyses is still justified.

With variations, accounts of violent ethnonational conflict on the part of sociobiologists appeal to the function of hostility toward or fear of out-groups for promoting in-group cohesion. As to why such cohesion is necessary, this is explained by reference to the survival value to humans of cooperation, thus raising a further question about why such cooperation should not extend beyond limited boundaries and why the boundaries are so remarkably divergent in extent (families, tribes, cities, regions, nations, religious communities, etc.) or, conversely, why xenophobia should not extend beyond very small groups of immediate dependents.

Sociobiologists addressing group conflict diverge in explaining these things.[3] Richard Alexander holds that competitiveness requires a certain blend of hostility and cooperation. Ian Vine suggests that the altruism required for cooperation must be tempered with "a weakly xenophobic tendency." Peter Meyer argues that "affectivity is a scarce resource" which can only extend to limited numbers of people. (He somehow picks the number thirty.) To my mind these explanations are strained efforts at hypothesis saving. Sociobiology may well play a role in respect of some aspects of ethnonational conflict—for instance, in accounting for why the young males who enthusiastically take up arms are overendowed with testosterone—but I suspect that the macrophenomenon itself is too culturally infused and historically specific to admit of useful biological explanation. *Pure laine* (as the more chauvinistic of Franco-Quebec nationalists refer to the stuff required to be a true Quebecer) is not easily interpreted as pure blood, nor old stock (the Anglo-Canadian analogue) as gene stock.

Core aspects of the late Frank Wright's application of Girard's theory of violence to Northern Ireland and some other places[4] apply equally to the situation of Quebec and English-speaking Canada: societies on the frontiers of major world empires; historic grievances to incite revenge; the absence of secular or religious candidates for scapegoating; and (as is seen in a 1998 declaration of Lucien Bouchard, then the premier of Quebec, that his government would ignore a forthcoming ruling of the Supreme Court of Canada about whether secession was constitutional)[5] lack of fear of overarching law. In Girardian theory such conditions yield a prediction of cycles of revenge-motivated violence. The problem is that since these conditions have been in place in Canada for some time and, indeed, more starkly in earlier times, the theory ought not to be predicting violence but retrodicting it.

The theory of human nature underlying Girard's perceptive accounts of how revenge takes on a life of its own—evidently applicable to several violence-ridden parts of the world today—crucially involves mimetic envy: "I want it because you have it." While experimental psychology seems to hold some evidence for such a theory, it is hard to see how it would apply holistically to large ethnic or national groups. It is sometimes alleged by Quebec nationalists that those in the culturally amorphous and dispersed parts of Canada outside of Quebec suffer "nation envy." My own experience has been that those in English-speaking Canada who have proclaimed its nationhood—I'm thinking of philosophers in the tradition of George Grant or political economists such as Mel Watkins or Abe Rotstein[6]—have more often elicited reactions by compatriots who disagree on this score of rebuff for the pretense than of alarm at threatened nationhood. Moreover, it is hard to think of an analogous object of envy on the part of Franco-Quebec.

Russell Hardin's rational decision approach to ethnic conflict is based on a broadly Hobbesist theory of human nature: individuals are primarily motivated to pursue narrowly self-interested ends by whatever means will likely achieve them. This typically renders cooperative behavior problematic, due to the intractability of the prisoners' dilemma. By contrast, when people find themselves "coordinated" in groups, the members of which are not in competition with one another and whose joint actions serve individual goals, this dilemma does not obtain. This is sometimes the case with ethnic or national groups, thus sustaining people's identification with them. Unfortunately, groups themselves are not infrequently in conflict, and this can result in violence.[7]

Hardin is largely concerned to offer an alternative account of violent ethnic or national conflicts to those that regard them as motivated by atavistic blood lust, and in this I believe he has succeeded. In the examples he gives, ordinary people are more often tragically caught up in violence than willing instigators of it. But beyond this insight, I find his account inadequate to account for nonviolence. Because coordinated groups are modeled on rational individuals in his sense, violence should result whenever there is competition between groups or even when there is perceived potential competition; since, as he notes, it will always be rational for any group to launch a preemptive strike against another group, cooperation among groups to preclude this will confront the prisoners' dilemma again.

Hardin himself does not seek a general explanation for how groups end up in violent conflict. Sometimes, group conflicts accidentally "tip" into violence, or violence is instigated by self-serving group leaders. He laments that people identify with national or ethnic groups at all (thus devoting a third of his book, *One for All*, to condemnation of communitarian philosophers, who see such identification as a source of value for individuals), and he describes group identification per se as the root of violence. What group identifications people have or how they identify with a group is of incidental interest to the theory.

It seems to me, however, that understanding how group conflicts can turn violent requires close attention to specific group identifications and the manners in which they identify. Inattention to such matters is one of the things that makes Hardin's treatment of Canada unsatisfactory. Hardin's main concern is to figure out what Quebec wants. He speculates that perhaps the sovereigntists are motivated by desire to preserve Franco-language and culture, but he wishes to resist this conclusion because he does not regard it rational. His preferred explanation is that Quebecers figure they can do economically better under the terms of the North American Free Trade Agreement as an independent country than as part of Canada. Even a cursory reading of Quebec history, at least beginning with the "Quiet Revolution" in the 1960s, should make it clear that a principal motive has been cultural and that free trade is a recent factor, embraced by some sovereigntists, resisted by others.

ELEMENTS OF VIOLENCE

I do not pretend that the accounts of violent ethnonational conflict based on theories of human nature that I have summarized exhaust the field. The aim is to demonstrate that while useful ideas are suggested by such accounts, they are of dubious application to the current Canadian situation. Theories of human nature applied to violent ethnonational conflict are also likely to be biased in a pessimistic direction. Because violent conflicts actually take place, such theories could hardly lead to the conclusion that this is foreign to human nature, and because violence is so widespread and persisting, it would be difficult to conclude that it is a deviation. Still, I do not think that philosophers addressing the topic need shun human nature theorizing altogether or embrace a purely constructivist stance toward the human condition. Rather, I believe that this issue can be sidestepped. Pro–human nature theorists might also be sorted into two categories, which I label "crude" and "sophisticated," in which the former strive to identify a set of dispositions toward just one sort of behavior (e.g., selfish, violent, altruistic, or pacific), whereas the latter look for complex dispositions that may be in tension with one another. The theories I've summarized probably admit of either crude or sophisticated interpretations.

Crude human nature theorizing most easily fits what I call a "lid on the pot" paradigm of explanations for violent ethnonational conflict. According to this paradigm, violence is seething beneath the surface of national life and will bubble forth unless forcibly confined. This is a common approach to violence in Eastern Europe, which was supposed to have been present from at least the time of the Ottoman Empire but contained by Soviet domination. In a contrasting, "combustion" paradigm, violent conflicts result from the coming together of independently innocuous elements that in combination have disastrous results. Obviously, violent conflict cannot take place if forcibly constrained, but in this paradigm absence of such constraint is simply one element that may come into combination with others. Combustion paradigmatic accounts are clearly compatible with strong anti–human nature theories. They are also compatible with sophisticated viewpoints on human nature. However, for the purpose of inhibiting (or containing or reversing) violent conflict, primary attention to the combustible elements suffices.

Assuming the combustion paradigm (and setting aside general philosophical and inductive, historical arguments that I believe can be given in its favor), I wish now to identify those combustible elements suggested to me by examination of places where violent ethnonational conflict has already taken place. These are a certain popular culture of enmity, economic conditions fostering malcontent and mean spiritedness, the absence of acceptable channels for pacific resolution of differences, and an appropriate spark. I shall summarize each of these and then apply them to the current situation in Canada.

In reading accounts of attitudes within the populations of conflict-torn parts of the world and conducting informal interviews in recent research trips to some of these places, I have tried to ascertain the character of ethnically hostile attitudes by identifying their phenomenological centers—that is, the core attitudes around which people made sense of their conflictual social worlds. I found no dearth of fear, vengefulness, and attitudes of superiority, sometimes verging on racism, but concluded that these figure more as causes, effects, or justifications for violence than as organizing principles of a violence-sustaining worldview. The candidate I favor is "blame." People immersed in relations of enmity view opposing groups as morally blameworthy for misfortunes they suffer in common with other members of their own group: economic hardship, frustrated political self-determination, erosion of their culture, and the like. With blame comes demonization of the other group and a sense of oneself as a victim. It is because blame has a moralistic dimension that people are able to endorse behavior that is dangerous to themselves and in normal circumstances would be seen as morally unacceptable.

Return to Hardin's theory serves to introduce what I see as the economic combustible element. His only concrete political prescription for avoiding ethnic or national strife is worldwide capitalist competition. Citing Adam Smith for authority, he says, "we make a better world by ignoring what kind of world we make and living for ourselves than if we concentrate first on the ethnic political structure of our world."[8] Echoing current neoliberal sentiments, Hardin advocates downsizing government, which he thinks will both promote generally beneficial free competition and remove an enticement for power-hungry leaders to whip up popular hatreds (namely to secure control of a strong state). I believe there is some room for doubt that unbridled capitalism has the potential currently claimed for it to create worldwide prosperity. More precisely, I see invisible hand and trickle-down rhetoric as little more than cynical rationalization for augmenting morally reprehensible privilege on the part of the already bloated rich. However, if general prosperity or even just economic security could be achieved, whether through laissez-faire capitalism or any other method, then one contributor to violence would be eliminated. I do not mean that economic conflict is the cause of violence, nor that religious, ethnic, national, or other forms of extraeconomic conflict would cease, but only that in the absence of economic hardship on the part of one or all parties, the conflicts would be easier to manage and violence less likely.

There is, however, a cultural dimension to capitalist competition that could still have fractious consequences. I am thinking of the political culture of what C. B. Macpherson called "possessive individualism," wherein people view their own and others' capacities as commodities to be bought and sold in a competitive market for the sake of limitless pursuit of consumer goods. This culture, Macpherson persuasively argued, promotes values of mean-spirited selfishness and greed.[9] Such values might militate against what Hardin calls coordination with others within a shared ethnic or national group, but it might also encourage such identification for the sake of competitiveness with those in other groups, with the result that the worst aspects of national or ethnic chauvinism and aggressive capitalism infuse one another. I believe that this is what has happened in Eastern Europe and the former Soviet Union.

Channels for peaceful confrontation of conflicts include an agreed-on body of law or a mutually acceptable process of arbitration. But they also include some subjective factors. One sometimes hears it said that the solution to group conflicts is for people to think of themselves as individuals and not as members of groups. While it is certainly true that a world of socially unencumbered individuals would minimize group conflicts, I consider such a prescription hopelessly unrealistic. Individuals importantly, if not exclusively, recognize themselves in terms of a variety of group identifications. However, no individual identifies with (or, if one wants to put the point more radically, is constituted by) one group alone. Somebody may identify with any combination of such things as an ethnicity, nationality, class, profession, gender, religion, linguistic community, generation, region, and so on, with varying and changing priorities. Members of groups made up of people who share highly prioritized identifications over time may have a range of attitudes toward other groups, from friendly feelings to indifference and hostility.

On a combustion paradigm, conflicts between such groups do not automatically turn to violence but may often be handled by peaceful negotiation. While almost any combination of possible objects of identification may be compatible with negotiation, certain objects must be kept out of an identifying cluster—namely, those required for negotiation itself. I am thinking, in particular, of geographic terrains physically inhabited by different groups and of political terrains wherein negotiation may take place. If the members of a group believe that exclusive domination of a territory or that preponderance of state power is integral to their very identities, this denies the terrains for peaceful negotiation, and violence is risked.

The elements of a violence prompting combustion so far listed are more contingent than those appealed to in crude human nature theories, but they figure in more systematic accounts than those often found in popular history—for instance, of the sort that could explain World War I just by reference to the assassination of Archduke Ferdinand. At the same time, such contingent precipitating events still do play a part, just as do sparks in an actual combustion. It is for this reason that when violence begins people are sometimes surprised with how quickly it spreads. Perhaps this lends plausibility to the lid on the pot paradigm.

THE SITUATION OF CANADA/QUEBEC

The point about sparks is best explained by turning to the Canadian case and the Aboriginal fact ignored in the earlier conference of philosophers.[10] Shortly before the 1995 Quebec referendum, the Cree announced that if Quebec left the confederation, they would remain. What if the vote in that referendum (decided by about 1 percent) had gone differently and, failing a compromise in the resulting negotiations (the track record of such negotiations has not been stellar), Quebec had announced secession? Cree lands are so extensive and rich in resources that it is likely that the Quebec government would have obliged them to remain within the new country, and if the Cree resisted, force might well have been employed. Violent encounters between native peoples and governments in Canada, in and out of Quebec, are not unprecedented.[11] Had the Cree called on the federal government for help, what would have happened? I remain optimistic that such a scenario would have drawn all parties back from the brink. But if other elements of a combustion are present this is just the sort of thing that can spark violence. The sociobiologists have at least underscored the point that violent behavior is not inimical to human comportment. Hardin well explains how violence can be an unintended consequence of seemingly benign antecedents, such as national commitments, and Girard reminds us that once begun, violence is fed by cycles of revenge.

My reading of the situation is that some measure of all the combustible elements listed earlier is present. That each is mixed with counteracting features and is not exactly full-blown gives one cause for hope, but that the elements exist at all is worrisome. Alarmists point to such things as jokes made by Anglophones and Francophones at each other's expense or jeers at the language in which the anthem is sung at sporting events as evidence of dangerously hostile cultural attitudes. Though distasteful, I do not think these things grave in themselves. Perhaps one thing that sociobiological or Girardian theories can help us to understand is why and how bonding rivalries involving chants, colors, and the like are so widespread and intense even among people who have a great deal in common (e.g., neighboring cities or schools). More troubling are attitudes of blame, which I identified as the phenomenological center of parties to violent conflict.

At the core of blame in Quebec is belief that English-speaking Canada is responsible for the erosion, or threatened erosion, of important parts of Quebec culture and especially the French language. Canadians outside of Quebec charge the latter with trying to break up the country. In all situations of conflict, cultures of blame have some objective basis, and this is no less true in the Canadian situation. But, also as in other places, blame grows out of proportion, becomes more diffuse, and comes to take on a central place in people's phenomenological fields. Thus, in both Quebec and the rest of Canada other threats to the French language and to Canadian unity, such as global and domestic economic threats, are often overlooked. I encounter people in my part of the country attributing all sorts of social and political problems to Quebec sovereigntists who could have little to do with them. The Quebec license plate slogan "*Je me souviens*" has come to refer not to religious and other traditional values, as originally intended, or even to the Plains of Abraham where British forces conquered Quebec in 1759, but to mistreatment of Quebec by *les anglais* in general. Not long after the 1996 referendum in Quebec, a major and mainstream English Canadian newspaper, the *Toronto Star*, featured a gruesome cartoon in which the sovereigntist premier of

Quebec at the time was depicted chopping off the tongue of a figure labeled "Anglophone." One hears of less violent but still analogous demonization of prominent federalists in Quebec.

I shall return to consideration of some matters of popular culture after addressing the topic of combustible economic conditions. Behind these conditions in the Canadian case is a vexing problem that nearly everyone grants has plagued the country since confederation. As in any federation made up of regions with special needs and more or less distinct cultures, but still requiring some measure of centralized organization and a central tax base to remain economically strong and to account for unevenness of benefits and opportunities, a continuing problem has been to find the right balance between centralization and decentralization. This problem is exacerbated in Canada due to its national complexity: if Quebec is treated like all the other provinces, it will not have sufficient powers to conduct its affairs in a way that is satisfactory to its majority Francophone population, but if Quebec is given special powers for this end, other provinces demand equal special treatment.

In recent years, the Business Council on National Issues (BCNI), an organization made up of the CEOs of the largest capitalist enterprises and a group that has given new life to conspiracy theory in the Canadian left, entered the long-standing debates on this question by recommending radical devolution of powers to Quebec and to all the other provinces. This is easy for the council to advocate since large capital has shown little interest in preserving safety nets for the economically disadvantaged, maintaining environmental controls or labor standards, or pursuing proactive countrywide economic plans aside from deficit reduction or tax relief—in short, the sorts of things that a strong central government is needed to do. The BCNI's intervention, echoed by conservative think tanks; a right-wing populist political party; the Canadian Alliance, recently formed from mainly Western-based conservative groupings; and wings of the traditional Progressive Conservative Party, reflects increasing neoliberal, deregulatory policies implemented by the federal government and several provinces, including Quebec, where the neoliberal wing of the PQ currently dominates its social democrats.[12] The ostensive promise of neoliberal economic policies is promotion of economic competitiveness, job creation, and the trickle down of wealth. As already indicated, I doubt that the policies have these effects and fear that they will, instead, create increasing economic hardship and insecurity for the overwhelmingly large majority of the population—fertile soil for general discontent and attitudes of hostility toward groups said to be the cause of one's troubles.

Following Macpherson, I earlier claimed that neoliberal economic practice and popularly disseminated theory contribute to possessive-individualist values. The BCNI's recommendation for devolution is attached by it to demands for provincial and regional autonomy. This contributes to the integration of these values with provincial and regional identifications and encourages people to think of the regional or national groups with which they identify as necessarily, even desirably, in competition with others. Furthermore, group identification itself can come to be viewed instrumentally, as a tool for individual competition. When mean-spirited and competitive economic values are linked with provincial, regional, or national rivalries, possessive individualism feeds "possessive nationalism," and yet another element conducive to violent combustion is present.

The third element to be discussed in the Canadian case is the absence of channels for peaceful resolution. Some channels still remain, but the traditional method of negotiation among political elites is, if not entirely closed off, at least suspect after dramatic failures of major federal government-led initiatives for a redistribution of provincial and federal powers in the Meech Lake Accord of 1987 and the Charlottetown Accord of 1992. Refusal to recognize the authority of the Supreme Court regarding matters pertaining to secession by the PQ with support of a large proportion of the Quebec public weakens the prospect for employing legal channels.

Remaining are more democratic, people-to-people encounters, in which there may be some ground for hope. I am not referring to referenda or to attempted love-ins like one just before the Charlottetown vote when the Liberal Party sent train loads of Canadians to Montreal to protest their affection. Rather, I am referring to occasional, if so far rare, encounters at which problems besetting the confederation are addressed by people who share interests cutting across the national divide—to advance the status of women, working people's interests, environmental concerns, religious convictions, and so on. Such activities have the potential to seek out and bring political pressure to bear for securing pacific channels in part just because their participants are not monolithically constituted in terms of specifically national interests.

As to possessive nationalism, we are most fortunate not to confront theocratic identifications. Nor are national identities as desperately fused to a land as in places such as Palestine. However, there are still exclusionary attitudes toward territory that, while involving geopolitical calculations, go beyond these to approach identity-determining attachments. On the Quebec side this is most evident in the case of the northern lands made objects of contest by conflict with the Cree and other Aboriginal peoples referred to earlier. At a gathering I attended in 1998 of political theorists from Quebec and Anglo Canada designed to find grounds for constructive dialogue, the question of whether Quebec borders could be a matter of negotiation, especially in the case of these lands, was the major sticking point in striving to reach a consensus.

From the side of Anglo Canada, I think an attitude of possessive nationalism is reflected in the common bumper sticker reading, "My Canada includes Quebec." Puzzlement over the meaning of this slogan prompts reflection about identity formation in Canada and Quebec. I am guided by the premise that national and ethnic identities are constructed, which means they are not fixed, and they are subject to influence by active intervention. This provides grounds for hope that the specifically cultural elements of a potential combustion can be counteracted, and it also gives philosophers something worthwhile to do other than playing the Owl of Minerva. However, construction can also be destructive.

I am thinking here of some journalistic approaches to national conflicts in Canada. One of these is reflected in a newspaper column by a prominent Anglo-Canadian journalist, Gwynne Dyer, around the time of the PQ's 1998 re-election: "Since its birth Canada has been plagued by two rival tribalisms, British and French." Luckily immigration has diluted at least one of the tribes (the British): "If Canada were a Balkan country, we . . . would be stuck with the ethnic groups and hatreds we started out with. . . . But we are a country of immigrants and that means we can change."[13] Now, as I understand each situation, Canada is indeed like the Balkans in some respects, one of them being that *neither* is correctly described as tribal. Rather, such rhetoric in the popular media itself a slur against tribally organized Aboriginal societies due to its modern connotation of atavistic hatred and violence—contributes to potentially self-generating anticipations of violence and to simplistic self-identification by antagonistic bonding: sporting event jeers and aggressive flag waving writ large.

The upside of construction is the possibility of reconstruction. What has been stitched together can be taken apart and reconstituted. I believe that something like this has happened in Ireland, where religious affiliations have shifted from being primary components of conflicting national identities to markers for political identifications—Loyalist and Republican—that have displaced them in this role. This did not of itself end the violence, but it meant, in accord with Frank Wright's neo-Girardian speculations, that with changing priorities in the relevant political metropolises (the United Kingdom and the Republic of Ireland) the sustaining bases of antagonistic nationalisms in Ulster began to wane. In his contribution to the 1979 conference of the Canadian philosophers, Francis Sparshott offered a line of reconstruction concerning Canada. He deplored the fusion of state and body politic in debates over confederation, suggesting that this represents an outmoded conception of sovereignty. With the breakup of empires, the divinely sanctioned absolute power of rulers became sovereign state control over territory.[14]

Along the same lines, but with a different emphasis, I am inclined to think that a root fusion to be challenged is that between "land" (as in "homeland" or "This land is my land" in the popular song) and "territory" (as in the spaces bounded by surveyors' markers, or urine), or in French the distinction between *terroir* and *territoire*. Assumption of such a fusion means that identification with a land requires exclusive sovereignty with respect to it or, conversely, defense of a territory becomes a point of national pride. Success in prying the notion of land and territory apart would open the door to conceptions of sharing a land or of reconceiving sovereignty to void it of the notion of exclusive domination.[15] In the Canadian case, it would create options for negotiation foreclosed as long as national identities are territorially infused.

ETHNIC AND CIVIC NATIONALISM/STATE AND NATION

Returning to the bumper sticker slogan, on the surface it could and probably usually does just mean "We Anglo-Canadians like Quebecers and don't want them to depart from the country," although it is also sometimes advanced in a threatening way. In any case, it is worth trying to figure out just what is feared to depart from what. A simple interpretation is that the slogan refers to the state of Canada and its substate component, the province of Quebec, and is thus a declaration against political secession. In a more statist society than Canada, such as the United States or France, where being part of a powerful and unified state is an important component of people's identities, such a conception might be strongly enough held to evoke passion. Such passion might also accompany an imperial identity that remembered the Plains of Abraham British victory, but this, too, is surely confined to very few people in contemporary Canada.

Perhaps the slogan is, rather, a declaration of Canadian nationhood. It could then be interpreted to mean "Quebec's being a part of the country is important to my Canadian national identity." This interpretation also seems strained to me. For one thing, as mentioned earlier, it supposes a stronger sense of Canadian nationhood than is likely found within the general population. Recognition of Quebec as a nation is also unlikely if, whether with benign or menacing intent, the sticker is displayed to indicate opposition to Quebec sovereigntists, since admission or rejection of Quebec nationhood has become definitive of one's stand on sovereignty.

The most likely situation is that people sporting the sticker do not know what it means beyond either an affirmation of friendship or a threat and that one reason for this is that the relation between Canadian nationhood and Canadian statehood is not clearly fixed in the popular mind. Those who level the "nation envy" charge at Anglo Canada would interpret this as a result of nonexistent nationhood. Though the topic is too large to defend here, I believe that such a charge is unjustified and that, broadly speaking, it makes sense to characterize Canada as a single state composed of three national groupings: Quebec, Canada outside Quebec, and the ensemble of Aboriginal nations, understanding that national sentiments admit of degrees of strength and granting that the concept is contested.[16] Conventional wisdom among theorists who can agree with this interpretation regarding Canada or any other bi- or multinational state is that people who confuse state and nation are either simply mistaken or are deliberately obfuscating the distinction for political purposes.[17] At the current juncture of Canada–Quebec relations, I suggest that this convention on the part of the engaged political theorists needs rethinking, and I shall shortly turn to this task, but first I wish to introduce a related effort in rethinking—namely, of the relation between civic and ethnic nationalism. In Canada this task is motivated by consideration of the tension between nationalism and multiculturalism.

Quebec is not homogeneously made up of people whose maternal language is French, but it includes as well an Anglo community and several communities of

"Allophones"—that is, those whose maternal language is neither English nor French. Anglophones and Allophones make up about 10 percent each of the total Quebec population. Also, there are minority Francophone populations in each of the provinces outside Quebec. In earlier times, those in and out of Quebec who were prepared to talk of a French nation in Canada saw Quebec as the center of this nation, whose members included all the Francophones in the country. Around the time of the first election of the PQ in 1976, when the prospect of secession became a thinkable option, reference to a French nation fell out of common discourse in Anglo Canada, while nationalists in Quebec began to think of Quebec alone as a nation. In addition to generating not a little resentment among Francophones outside Quebec (who felt betrayed by the exclusion), this shift left the thorny question of the status of the Anglo- and Allophones unresolved.

The tension was illustrated on the eve of the narrow defeat of the second Quebec referendum on sovereignty (in 1992) when the then premier of the province, Jacques Parizeau, publicly described the defeat as the combined result of threats of economic reprisal by English Canadian–based big capital and the vote of the Anglophones and Allophones. While not an inaccurate report regarding the breakdown of the vote (or regarding the threats of capital), in context, Parizeau's comments reflected the sort of dangerous culture of victimhood referred to earlier wherein national self-determination is not only denied by *les anglais*, in and out of Quebec, but also by Allophones in the Province, who are branded enemies within. Thus construed, Parizeau's comments highlighted a problem familiar to all nationalistic secessionist movements of this century: what stance to take toward the minority groups within a majority nationality. Thankfully, Parizeau's tone of resentment has not found expression in ethnic cleansing–type rhetoric on the part of the PQ, which instead has projected a nation-state with two official languages, French and English, where, however, Allophones are to send their children to French-speaking public schools and thus eventually assimilate, at least linguistically, to the Francophone majority. But there remains no consensus about how to conceptualize the national/ethnic relations in the province.

One line of thought taken up by some Quebec intellectuals draws on the work of David Miller and Yael Tamir, among others, who have introduced the notion of "civic" or "liberal" nationalism into the general debates over this topic. According to a strong version of civic nationalism, loyalties of Quebecers would be as citizens who share commitment to liberal-democratic political and legal institutions.[18] The shortcoming of civic nationalism in this stark form (not embraced by Miller and Tamir themselves) is that it risks losing touch with national sentiments of the Francophone majority, whose support for sovereignty has been motivated by linguistic and other cultural concerns rather than simply civic values, which in any case are currently embedded in the federal constitution.

Successful confrontation in theory of the unstable relation between ethnicity and civility in national arenas would help to provide a perspective from which to resist development of a full-blown and combustible element of blame. I thus concur with the organizing theme of a recent collection of essays on nationalism published by the *Canadian Journal of Philosophy* described by its (Quebec sovereigntist) editors, Jocelyne Couture, Kai Nielsen, and Michel Seymour, as the "supersession" of the ethnic/civic nationalism distinction.

These philosophers identify as pure types the civic nationalism of Ernest Renan, for whom the nation is primarily an association in which people are bound together by common commitment to political values, and ethnic nationalism, of the sort extolled by Johann Gottfried Herder, based on language, culture, and tradition.[19] As the editors note, no stark examples of these pure types can be found, and all theorists addressing the subject, including Renan and Herder, advance nuanced views, albeit ones that place their emphases on one or the other of the ethnic or civic poles in their attempts to define "nationhood." For example, Miller, Tamir, and Will Kymlicka identify shared ethnic or cultural national cores (variously described by them) that are embedded within political societies with their own, uniquely civic values.[20] Couture et al. reverse this characterization and see nations as "political communities" that "very often" contain majority and sometimes also "minority nationalities" within them.[21] Dominique Schnapper maintains that, not withstanding the unavoidable tension between them, civic and ethnic attitudes are jointly necessary elements of any national state.[22]

Perhaps a universally applicable definition of "nation" or cognates can be articulated and defended, but I have the impression that putative attempts to date are usually tailored to local circumstances and aims. This was clearly the case of Renan and Herder, who had postrevolutionary France and the emerging Germany in mind. Tamir makes this observation, noting Kymlicka's effort to make room for limited national rights within Canadian liberal individualism and Miller's concern to promote nation-friendly welfare politics in the United Kingdom.[23] Her own efforts, as she acknowledges, grow out of her national experiences (in Israel), and the effort of Couture, Nielsen, and Seymour is explicitly motivated by the aim of defending a pluricultural vision of a sovereign Quebec. Thus, while I shall frame my own run at the "nation question" in general terms, I have more confidence about it regarding Canada/Quebec than regarding other places.

In his contribution to the 1979 Canadian Philosophical Association conference on Confederation, Charles Taylor argued that the virtue of national cultures is that they provide "a horizon of meaning, which can only be provided by some allegiance, group membership [or] cultural tradition," which in the modern world, where people's identities are in flux, is required as a base from which they can give meaning to their lives.[24] In the same conference, Sparshott offered a more prosaic explanation of the same type: "My nation is defined by those with whom I feel at home, not having to think about what I do, not having to explain myself. . . . My nation, like my family, consists of those with whom I am presumed by myself and others not to be strangers."[25]

Taylor entitled his contribution "Why Do Nations Have to Become States?" because he saw a tendency for people sharing national identifications to attempt securing them and gaining international recognition by means of statehood. In the light of persuasive arguments by recent historians that nations, states, and hence nation-states have diverse origins, in some of which not only statehood but nationhood is "constructed,"[26] Taylor's thesis should not be taken as a general causal one. This does not mean, however, that determination (or at least preparedness) to defend the sorts of cultural contexts that Taylor and Sparshott describe plays no role in the construction and maintaining of states. The advantage of a state for this purpose is that it can use legal means to protect, enhance, or promote a shared culture—for instance, in language policies, education, and cultural funding programs. Arguably, then, people for whom aspects of a culture are important will be at least disposed to favor state measures to preserve them, while, conversely, attempts to force a state on people with no such dispositions will secure popular loyalty (if at all) only with difficulty, as was exemplified in several parts of the late communist world.

For this reason, articulation of an intimate connection between nation and state is needed. Not all cultural participations are as central to the popular identities (or quests for identity) that Sparshott and Taylor describe, and people for whom such participation is central are not always in demographic, economic, or geographic circumstances that make statehood a realistic option. But when the cultural features are central and the circumstances are apt, state support for the shared cultural identities will be an attractive option. The presence of this option is what, in my view, distinguishes nations from ethnic groups and hence multinationalism from multiculturalism. I digress to expand on this point since it is especially important in Canada, which in 1982 constitutionally entrenched commitment to multiculturalism and which includes both in Quebec and elsewhere a large number of diverse ethnic communities.

The upside of official multiculturalism has been to afford people of other than Anglo and Franco origins legitimization and sometimes resources for maintaining aspects of their unique cultures and to resist the ethnic chauvinism accompanying alternative, "melting pot" policies. This does not mean that ethnic chauvinism is absent. In English-speaking Canada proclamations of commitment to multiculturalism, especially outside a few large urban centers, do not go much beyond toleration for occasional folk festivals and mask a fair measure of continuing Anglo—indeed, Anglo-Protestant—chauvinism. Franco-chauvinism in Quebec is exacerbated by the fact that from the late 1960s and 1970s, federalist political leaders have appealed to multiculturalism to characterize Franco communities, both inside and outside Quebec, as one ethnic group among the many others in the Canadian "cultural mosaic." Far from dissolving Franco-Quebec nationalist sentiments, this stance has fueled the fire of its most chauvinistic adherents—those for whom to be a true Quebecer is not just to speak French ("unaccented") but to be of Franco-Quebec lineage (the *pure laine* enthusiasts).

Standing against such chauvinists are those, such as intellectuals including the editors of the aforementioned collection and members of various social movements in the province, who envisage a Quebec made up of people from several ethnic and national origins but self-identified as Quebecers, competent and willing to function in French as the main language of public affairs, committed to Quebec's political and juridical systems, and respectful of the main inherited traditions of its majority.[27] Pitting multiculturalism against nationalism can only impede the efforts of the nonchauvinists in the Quebec context where the majority sees itself not just as an ethnic group but as a nation. The theoretical problem is to identify in what this nationhood consists. I submit that among its defining characteristics is the realistic ability, as well as the preparedness of people otherwise culturally identified, to seek statehood to preserve and promote those aspects of their culture that are important to them if statehood is deemed required by them for this purpose.[28]

A demographic precondition for statehood is that the resulting state includes a significant majority committed to preserving the relevant cultural features that motivate its formation. Ethnic minorities in the resulting state will likely constitute a spectrum, from those who have come to identify with at least some aspects of the majority culture, to others who are prepared to support and even politically identify with the (dominant) nation-state provided its offices and benefits are open to them, and it includes tolerant, nonchauvinistic attitudes on the part of the majority, to still others who are in varying degrees dissatisfied with such a development and at best prepared to accept it only grudgingly and of necessity. Such a definition does not by itself entail that any nation has an unconditional *right* to statehood. For instance, intolerance and the prospect of persisting diminished opportunities for ethnic minorities should defeat claim to such a right. But if, on any of several philosophical-normative grounds or even just pragmatic-political ones, it is thought that people constituting a nation on this conception ought, *cateris paribus*, to be accommodated,[29] then either state status or something that would equally serve national ends are legitimate options.

Statehood, itself, breeds and sustains cultural dimensions, some of which, such as statism, are pernicious, but others, such as acknowledgment of the equal rights of citizens (when liberal states are in question), are generally to be encouraged. Values attached to the specifically state-related functions of passing and enforcing laws are at the core of what are commonly designated the civic values, such as respect for the rule of law and toleration of different life plans among citizens, as long as they also conform to the civic values. Civic values may thus become part of a citizen's cultural identification. They differ from prepolitical cultural values in part by always involving a normative commitment, which, in accord with Wayne Norman, I agree not all national or other ethnic identifications do.[30] However, while adherence to civic values may become as it were "new" parts of a person's national identity, I doubt that they can bear no relation at all to those aspects of preexisting cultural identifications or at least of those of them that involve shared values as well as identifications.

It is from such identifications that the civic values gain their motivating force; if they were unrelated to or at odds with cultural identifications, the disposition to statehood for the purpose of protecting or advancing the latter would be counteracted. Leaving it to political-cultural historians to evaluate them, I advance as an illustrative hypothesis that the particular form of participatory democracy of ancient Athens was thus underwritten, so to speak, by some preexisting mores, notwithstanding the tragedians' depiction of conflicts between the utterly old and the utterly new ways (perhaps these conflicts would not be altogether tragic if there were no bases for simultaneous mutual attractions and repulsions). The sexist exclusions of that form of democracy is also found in already existing cultural grounds.

Analogous comments can be made about nondemocratic state forms and the liberal-democratic civic values of our times. The reason that overlapping consensuses can be achieved among people with different life goals in a liberal democracy in this hypothesis is that there are antecedent bases for agreement. Liberal-democratic societies, such as France and the United States, the political forms of which originated in revolutions, are sometimes portrayed by their champions as having completely cast off the old moralities and identifications, but such claims do not explain differences in the character and deployment of civic values even between these countries, for which one needs to appeal (though not, of course, exclusively) to prerevolutionary cultural as well as economic and political differences. Against this sort of theoretical background Taylor is able to show how Franco-Quebec and Anglo-Canadian political values can overlap, though expressed and interpreted differently because of the different cultures from which they arose (communal and individualist, respectively).[31] It is thus that nation and state are intimately associated.

Sparshott devoted a portion of his intervention at the confederation conference to the notion of "sovereignty," or the overwhelming exercise of power within a territory, insulated from constraint, which he portrayed as an anachronistic throwback to the thinking of premodern empires and at odds both with the needs of the body politic of individuals and with national collectives.[32] Not only does this ring true from a prescriptive point of view, but it is clear that state sovereignty has never been complete and that it is becoming less so. The recurring constitutional crises in Canada, like similar problems in all multinational states, are examples of the state's inability in such situations to provide cultural protection of support to everyone's satisfaction. Even mononational states are limited in their powers in the world's many federated countries, none of which, to my knowledge, is immune from gray and contested areas between and among local and federal state authorities. No state has had total control over all the relations within it and between itself and extrastate institutions internationally. With the growing force of global economic agencies, large areas of state sovereignty are being eroded de facto, and de jure state sovereignty is giving way to international laws and institutions, as in the case of the European

Union. Together these considerations suggest that statehood, far from being complete and insulated, is a matter of degree.

Assuming that I've got them more or less right, attending to these two phenomena—the interpenetration of civic and cultural values and the degrees of statehood—suggests places to focus on to confront elements of a potentially violent combustion in Canada. The most obvious implication concerns the absence of channels for seeking compromise solutions. Recall that the most severe of such impediments is encountered when protection of national or other identities is thought to require full national control over a state, in the extreme case involving a fusion of national and state identifications. Such fusion can be counteracted by acknowledging the intimate connection between state and nation but emphasizing the instrumental nature of the state's role in support of national identifications and the variability in a state's sovereignty. When the subordinate role of the state with respect to national concerns is highlighted, and it is recognized that sovereignty need not be absolute but can be partitioned and shared in a number of ways, attention can be turned to the practical questions about what form of association can best serve all relevant national interests. I favor some form of asymmetrical federalism but recognize other options.[33] On the principle that pragmatics is a good antidote to ideology, such questioning has the potential to weaken what I earlier labeled possessive nationalism.

To the extent that demonization of a hostile other derives in part from feelings of political impotence, opening spaces for negotiation over sharing power within a common state or between (quasi-) independent ones should help to direct energies in constructive ways, thus addressing a second combustible element by diffusing what was earlier labeled a phenomenological center of blame. In addition, the orientation here prescribed dictates dialogue, initially to strive for mutual understanding of simultaneously divergent and convergent values and then to seek ways of highlighting and drawing up common policy on the basis of convergence. This is what Taylor calls a "politics of recognition,"[34] and it seems to me that even embarking on such a path will help to counteract or forestall development of enmity-defined self-identifications. Such an undertaking may be hard to get going, especially if a measure of enmity already exists, but I believe it realistic if one encourages looking first not at contradictory statements at state-level power politics, but at values in popular cultures to find convergent paths.

If such processes are hard to start, they ought to be progressively easier to pursue once started, as mutual understanding deepens and successful joint action breeds enthusiasm. One objection to such a strategy is that it would stand no chance of success if, looking into the souls of a dialoging partner, one was repulsed by what is seen. This might sometimes happen, of course, but I maintain in the case of Quebec and Anglo Canada that demonizing mythology is not at all reflective of general popular values on either side. A weightier objection is that by bringing matters of national identity into the political arena, they become politicized in a pejorative sense as differences are exaggerated to stake out bargaining positions and political leaders whip up nationalist antagonisms. In response to this objection, it should first be noted that national matters are already part of the political landscape in Canada—indeed, often dominating it—and simply declaring that they be taken off the agenda is not a viable option.

An alternative proposal to that of taking national concerns out of politics is to turn efforts at national recognition against a certain way of conducting politics. This was the response of Sparshott, whose perspicacious observations on this point merit quotation in full:

> It has been said that the idea of a nation is cultural rather than political. . . . But that view seems to rest on the equation of politics with the distribution of powers, on the [exclusionary] sovereignty model [which is] to degrade the notion of politics and thus unwittingly to degrade the quality of public affairs. Of the alternative notions of what politics is, interest brokerage likewise has no special place for nationhood, though national interests could be set alongside commercial and other interests as recognizable participants in negotiations; but one could argue that this view of politics also, equating formal public interactions with trading relations, reflects and promotes a degraded view of humanity. But if we equate politics with the joint conduct of affairs in certain specifiable conditions, the nation becomes a *prima facie* political entity as consisting of those who have most joint affairs to conduct.[35]

In the perspective sketched here in which nation and state interpenetrate, Sparshott's concern that national questions not be regarded as entirely extrapolitical is accommodated, and if, in addition, the notion of sovereignty is relaxed and nation-regarding politics are carried on in a pragmatic way, there is an opening for the political activity as engagement in public affairs he calls for.[36]

What is more, current "specifiable conditions" of the main national groupings in Canada, both inside and outside Quebec, include an overriding problem— namely, that effective power to engage in collective action in or between any of them is being diminished due to global economic changes that take decision-making power over economic and social priorities out of Canadian hands. One reaction to this situation, unfortunately largely pursued by both federal and provincial political leaders (including in Quebec) is to try playing the neoliberal game: signing on to "free" trade agreements, reducing social services to cut taxes and remove constraints from profit-seeking entrepreneurs, foregoing national planning, and so on.

This is not the place to defend the claim that such a strategy is shortsighted for a small country like Canada. At best, it could only succeed in making some individuals rich or richer, and it involves the sort of brokerage politics Sparshott warns against, wherein regions, provinces, and national groupings within the country are played off against one another in efforts of global economic competition. It also encourages the possessive individualist values, which I described earlier, to contribute to the economic element of potentially violent combustion. An alternative strategy is to encourage joint action between Quebec and the rest

of Canada to cooperate in protecting institutions and practices traditionally valued as important parts of their national characters—for instance, linguistic and related cultural practices in Quebec and a culture in Anglo Canada that, by contrast
to its southern neighbor, is more egalitarian and less aggressively individualistic.
To the extent that such specifically national appeals are to commitments that are
not up for sale but are involved in people's national identities, this strategy therefore has the potential to counter yet another combustible element.

NATIVE PEOPLES

Earlier I suggested that one avenue for reconciling differences is direct interaction between relevant groups of people in and outside Quebec. I wish now to conclude with a prescription for what, as a first step or at least an essential component of any step, such groups should do. This is to address the concerns of the
third national grouping in Canada/Quebec, the Inuit and First Nations Peoples.

The publication in 1996 of the Report of a Royal Commission on Aboriginal
Peoples, which, backed up by a wealth of historical and other data, prescribes
ways that Aboriginal peoples could exercise appropriate self-determination,[37] offers an excellent occasion to put this question prominently on the agenda of any
such discussions—to which native people themselves should be party whenever
feasible. There is also a strong pragmatic incentive for resolving this issue—
namely, to extinguish the spark for violence referred to earlier. The "Indian question" is not going to go away. Land claims will persist. Canadians should not forget, either, that Aboriginal interventions have twice had important impacts on
constitutional debates and upset the plans of white politicians: first when the sole
Aboriginal member of the Manitoba legislature, Elija Harper, single-handedly
blocked that province's required endorsement of the proposal for a redistribution
of provincial and federal powers in the Meech Lake Accord and then when the
Assembly of First Nations (the umbrella group of First Nation and Innuit peoples
in Canada) withheld support for the second run at such a scheme in a countrywide
referendum over the Charlottetown Accord.

James Tully, among others (including the authors of the Royal Commission
Report), has made out a good case that models exist within Aboriginal history
and communities from which the rest of Canada may learn important lessons
relevant to Canada–Quebec relations. The notion of shared sovereignty is not
foreign to native political culture as it is to those inherited from Europe. In addition, there are lessons to be learned from native peoples about alternative
ways of regarding the relations of land or *terroir* and territory, state and nation,
and ethnicity and citizenship.[38]

At the very least a politics of national recognition should be a three-way matter. If, instead of playing the "Indian card" in a power-political way, people from
inside and outside Quebec, federalist and sovereigntist, jointly worked for just

settlement of Aboriginal demands, this could help to break down mutual suspicion. People who work together on a common project tend to grow together.[39] What is more, it should be noted that such a project has morality on its side. Aboriginal peoples in Canada account for less than 3 percent of the population, yet they continue to marshal sufficiently widespread popular support and sympathy that politicians cannot for long ignore them. I attribute this to the moral strength of their wish to extract themselves from the terrible conditions imposed on them.

Living up to moral responsibilities in this matter should have two more consequences relevant to avoiding the Bosnification of the country. First, the task requires challenging possessive individualist economic policies and culture. Ovid Mercredi, former head of the Assembly of First Nations, was right to announce, shortly before stepping down from that post, that he saw neoliberal policies of the Ministry of Finance as graver threats to Aboriginal aspirations than those of the Department of Indian Affairs. Moreover, not withstanding the sad fact that native peoples are sometimes driven by desperation to economic practices out of keeping with their traditions, we have something to learn from these traditions, which embody alternative values to possessive individualism. Writing with reference to Aborigenes of Australia, Ross Poole makes the apt point that in this regard Aboriginal attitudes toward their lands is in keeping with a normal stance of all peoples which is currently obscured by neoliberal rhetoric and practice: "The principle [of national sovereignty] has played an enormous role in the past two hundred years and continues to do so. If it has not been much discussed in much philosophy and political theory, this is because of the dominance of a narrowly economic understanding of the relationship between people and their physical environment."[40]

The effort should also help to combat intolerance generally. Recent scholarship on racism has been making out a good case that it and analogous forms of extreme intolerance have origins in the abysmal treatment of Aboriginal peoples during the campaigns of European colonial expansion.[41] As well as being culturally and physically genocidal, these campaigns set in motion psychodynamic processes among the Europeans and their descendants comparable to sexism in their tenacity and reach. Coming to grips with original and continuing degradation of the Aboriginal peoples both prompts and requires a self-critical attitude that is itself essential to a culture of tolerance and mutual respect. In this view, working together finally to retrieve the well-being and dignity of Native peoples in Canada is required to exorcise a demon that could otherwise drive it down a path nobody in the country wants to take.

NOTES

This contribution is modified from the presidential address to the Canadian Philosophical Association's 1998 annual meeting. Non-Canadian readers should be under no illusion that the contribution expresses anything approaching a consensus among Canadian political philosophers, including among those who provided me with useful feedback for revision of the address—namely, Derek Allen, Gregory Baum, G. A. Cohen, Kai Nielsen, Francis Sparshott, and Robert Ware, to whom thanks are due.

1. Proceedings of the conference were published in Stanley G. French, ed., *Confederation: Philosophers Look at Canadian Confederation/La Confédération canadienne: Qu'en pensent les philosophes?* (Montreal: Canadian Philosophical Association, 1979). Charles Taylor's contribution, "Why Do Nations Have to Become States?" was reproduced in his *Reconciling the Solitudes: Essays on Canadian Federalism and Nationalism* (Montreal: McGill-Queen's University Press, 1993), essay 3 (references are to the latter publication). Examples of subsequent publications (from among may) pursuing the same themes are *Philosophiques*, Numéro Spécial, *Une Nation peut-elle se donner la constitution de son choix,* dir. Michel Seymour, 19, no. 2 (Automne 1992); Joseph H. Carens, ed., *Is Quebec Nationalism Just? Perspectives from Anglophone Canada* (Montreal: McGill-Queen's University Press, 1995).

2. The results of some of this research are summarized in my "Group Hatreds and Democracy," in *Liberalism and Its Practice,* ed. Dan Avnon and Avner de-Shalit (London: Routledge, 1999), 127–45.

3. See the essays in Vernon Reynonds, Vincent Falger, and Ian Vine, eds., *The Sociobiology of Ethnocentrism: Evolutionary Dimensions of Xenophobia, Discrimination, Racism and Nationalism* (London: Croom Helm, 1987).

4. Frank Wright, *Northern Ireland: A Comparative Analysis* (Dublin: Gill & MacMillan, 1987) and *Two Lands on One Soil* (Dublin: Gill & MacMillan, 1993). René Girard's classic statement of his theory is *Violence and the Sacred,* trans. Patrick Gregory (Baltimore: Johns Hopkins University Press, 1977).

5. Shortly after the premier's declaration, the court predictably determined that secession is not constitutional but that if a clear majority of Quebecers opted for it, the rest of Canada would be well advised to negotiate over the issue. The content of this reference, Quebec's ex ante reaction, and the escalation of political intervention by the court have been matters of debate in Canada. See the essays in Barbara Cameron, ed., *The Supreme Court, Democracy, and Quebec Secession* (Toronto: Lorimer, forthcoming).

6. The best-known (Anglo-) Canadian nationalist philosopher was George Grant; see his *Lament for a Nation: The Defeat of Canadian Nationalism* (Toronto: McClelland & Stewart, 1965). Mel Watkins and Abe Rotstein are Canadian economists who in 1968 authored a report commissioned by the federal government (*Foreign Ownership and the Structure of Canadian Industry*) that became a touchstone for a generation of intellectuals and activists campaigning for policies to protect the Canadian economy and culture from U.S. domination. The flavor of this left-nationalist perspective may be sampled in a collection of journalistic essays by Watkins, *Madness and Ruin* (Toronto: Between the Lines, 1992).

7. Russell Hardin, *One for All: The Logic of Group Conflict* (Princeton, N.J.: Princeton University Press, 1995); I have critically reviewed this book in *The Canadian Journal of Philosophy* 27, no. 4 (December 1997): 571–94.

8. Hardin, *One for All,* 179.

9. C. B. Macpherson's major explication of possessive individualism is *The Political Theory of Possessive Individualism: Hobbes to Locke* (Oxford: Clarendon, 1962).

10. It is gratifying to report that at its 1998 annual meetings, the Canadian Philosophical Association undertook to organize a countrywide conference probably in 2000 on philosophical issues regarding Aboriginal self-government.

11. Within the last decade provincial police have engaged in armed combat with Aboriginal groups in British Columbia, Ontario, and Quebec. In 1970 Quebec was put under federal military control, with tanks in the streets of Montreal, when then Prime Minister Pierre Eliot Trudeau claimed to have discovered an "apprehended insurrection."

12. Ed Finn addresses provincial reactions to the "BCNI Agenda," *Canadian Forum* (May 1998): 6–8.

13. Gwynne Dyer, "How the 'New' Francophones Will Save Canada," *The Globe and Mail*, 28 March 1998, D3.

14. Francis Sparshott, "Nation and Sovereignty—Reflection on Two Concepts," in French, ed., *Confederation*, 107–15.

15. This notion was independently suggested to me with reference to Israel by the unlikely allies Emil Fackenheim and Asmi Bishara.

16. I explain and defend my version of Canadian "trinationalism" in "The Case of Canada/Quebec: A National Perspective," in *Diversity and Community: A Critical Reader*, ed. Philip Alperson (London: Blackwell, 2000).

17. The importance of keeping the notions of "state" and "nation" distinct was a theme in several of the contributions to the 1979 conference—for instance, Stanley Ryerson, "The Issue Is Equality," French, ed., *Confederation*, 161–65. More recently Robert Ware has underlined the distinction (relabeled "nation" and "nationality" by him) in "Nations and Social Complexity," in *Rethinking Nationalism*, ed. Jocelyne Couture, Kai Nielsen, and Michel Seymour, suppl. vol. 22 of the *Canadian Journal of Philosophy* (Calgary: University of Calgary Press, 1996): 133–57, at 134–42.

18. Yael Tamir, *Liberal Nationalism* (Princeton, N.J.: Princeton University Press, 1993); David Miller, *On Nationality* (Oxford: Clarendon, 1995). Closer to a stark form of civic nationalism is the "constitutional patriotism" advocated by Jürgen Habermas, *The New Conservatism: Cultural Criticism and the Historian's Debate* (Cambridge, Mass.: MIT Press, 1989). See the essay, "Historical Consciousness and Post-Traditional Identity."

19. Couture et al., eds., *Rethinking Nationalism*, 2–4.

20. Kymlicka explains his version of this view in, among other places, *Liberalism, Community, and Culture* (Oxford: Clarendon, 1989); see essay 7. Tamir and Miller's explications are in the books cited in note 18. In Canada, a collection of essays largely organized around the viability of civic nationalism (or "liberal nationalism," as Yael labels the viewpoint) is François Blais, Guy Laforest, and Diane Lamoureux, dirs., *Libéralismes et nationalismes* (Quebec: Presses de l'Université Laval, 1995); a popular expression of civic nationalism may be seen in *La Charte d'un Québec populaire* (Montréal: Solidarité populaire Québec, 1994).

21. Couture et al., eds., *Rethinking Nationalism*, editors' introduction, 37–39 and n. 46. They draw on an article explicating this point of view by Michel Seymour, "Une Conception sociopolitique de la nation," *Dialogue* 37, no. 3 (Summer, 1998): 435–71.

22. Dominique Schnapper, "Beyond the Opposition: Civic Nation vs. Ethnic Nation," in Couture et al., *Rethinking Nationalism*, 219–34.

23. Yael Tamir, "Theoretical Difficulties in the Study of Nationalism," in Couture et al., *Rethinking Nationalism*, 65–92, at 78–79.

24. Taylor, "Why Do Nations Have to Become States?"; see 46.

25. Francis Sparshott, "Nation and Sovereignty: Reflections on Two Concepts," in French, ed., *Confederation*, 107–15, at 111 (italics in the original omitted). Taylor and Sparshott describe language as a central prerequisite for fulfilling these functions, while

allowing for other shared cultural features, but neither assumes that a common language per se provides the needed horizon or family feeling, due to the infusion even of the same language with alternative cultural associations. In the view of Will Kymlicka, national and other "cultural heritages" are important because they provide people with a "context of choice" or a "cultural structure" through which they can become aware of "the options available to them, and intelligently examine their value" in adopting life plans. See *Liberalism*, essay 8, at 165. This yields a third explanation for why people might, justifiably, wish to preserve national and related cultures, but it is a weaker justification than that of Taylor or Sparshott. For all three theorists cultural identifications are means to things important to the individual—to lead a meaningful life, to feel at home, and to make informed choices—but one might say that the first two of these goals are more intimately or intrinsically related to their cultural "means" than is the third.

26. I am thinking of the work of Benedict Anderson, *Imagined Communities: Reflections on the Origin and Spread of Nationalism* (New York: Verso, 1983), and Eric Hobsbawm, *Nations and Nationalism since 1780* (Cambridge: Cambridge University Press, 1992).

27. One example is a coalition of churches, labor, and other social movements, Solidarité Populaire Québec. See its charter referred to in n. 20.

28. In this I disagree with Robert Ware's denial that potential statehood is required for something to be a nation ("Nations and Social Complexity," 141), though I am otherwise in sympathy with his holistic approach to such social phenomena as nations.

29. The arguments of Taylor and Sparshott have been summarized here earlier. Kymlicka and Tamir defend a presumptive right to national self-determination on liberal-individualistic bases. The pragmatic argument is that not to seek such accommodation will guarantee perpetual fractious relations. It should be noted that a presumptive right to statehood can be overridden by practical as well as moral considerations. Thus, the objection to this right that it could not be exercised by all the nations of the world because there is not enough room is beside the point. Whether realistic conditions for statehood are available to a people who wish it is sometimes a matter of sheer luck. The conclusion to draw from this point is not that therefore there is something amiss about the aspiration to statehood but that when this view is unrealistic, alternative means should be sought to accommodate that which motivates the aspiration. Relaxing sovereignty requirements of states should help in such endeavors.

30. Wayne Norman, "The Ideology of Shared Values: A Myopic Vision of Unity in the Multi-nation State," in Carens, ed., *Is Quebec Nationalism Just?* 137–59.

31. Charles Taylor, *Reconciling the Solitudes* (Montreal: Queen's-McGill Universities Press, 1993), chaps. 7, 8, and 9.

32. Sparshott, "Nation and Sovereignty," 107–8, 113–14.

33. I defend asymmetrical federalism in "The Case of Canada/Quebec." Among Anglo-Canadian political theorists, Alan Cairns articulates such a view in "Constitutional Change and the Three Equalities," in *Options for a New Canada,* ed. Ronald L. Watts and Douglas M. Brown (Toronto: University of Toronto Press, 1991), 77–102. See also a post-mortem of the Charlottetown Accord vote by members of a group of Toronto-based theorists in the *Canadian Forum* 71, no. 815 (December 1992).

34. Charles Taylor, "The Politics of Recognition," in *Multiculturalism: Examining the Politics of Recognition,* ed. Amy Gutmann (Princeton, N.J.: Princeton University Press, 1994): 25–73.

35. Sparshott, "Nation and Sovereignty," 111.

36. Sparshott is here implicitly challenging a popular view famously expressed by Benjamin Constant according to which engaged, community-based politics had, for better or worse, been superseded in the modern world by delegated and individual-regarding politics. See "The Liberty of the Ancients Compared with That of the Moderns," in *The Political Writings of Benjamin Constant* (New York: Beacon, 1988; from a speech given in 1819), 309–28.

37. *Report of the Royal Commission on Aboriginal Peoples* (Ottawa: Canadian Communication Group, 1996).

38. James Tully, *Strange Multiplicity: Constitutionalism in an Age of Diversity* (Cambridge: Cambridge University Press, 1995). For a succinct statement of Tully's approach, see, too, his "A Just and Practical Relationship between Aboriginal and Non-Aboriginal People of Canada," in *Canadian Politics,* 3d ed., ed. James Bickerton and Alain Gagnon (Peterborough, Canada: Macmillan, 1999).

39. I take it as a hopeful sign that intellectuals who actively intervene in the constitutional debates concur on the importance of addressing the Aboriginal question. Some examples are Tony Hall, "Aboriginal Issues and the New Political Map of Canada," in *"English Canada" Speaks Out,* ed. J. L. Granatstein and Kenneth McNaught (Toronto: Doubleday Canada, 1991), 122–40; Michel Seymour, "Le Nationalism Québécois et la question autochtone," in *Manifeste des intellectuels pour la souvereineté,* ed. Michel Sarra-Bouret (Montréal: Fides, 1995), 75–99; Henri Dorion, "Au delà de la Dialectique majorité/minorité: La Voie non gouvernmentale à la convivialité," in *L'État et les minorités,* ed. Jean Lafontant (Sanit-Boniface, Canada: Éditions du Blé, 1992), 187–99; and Peter Russell, "Aboriginal Nationalism and Quebec Nationalism: Reconciliation through Fourth World Decolonization," in *Constitutional Forum* 8, no. 4 (Summer 1997): 110–18. Readers acquainted with the political-theoretical landscape in Canada will know just how diverse this list is in terms of the authors' political, philosophical, and national orientations.

40. Ross Poole, "An Australian Perspective," in Couture et al., eds., *Rethinking Nationalism,* 407–38.

41. Tully makes this case in *Strange Multiplicities,* as do several other contemporary scholars, including Theodore Allen, *The Invention of the White Race* (New York: Verso, 1994); see also David Theo Goldberg, *Racist Culture: Philosophy and the Politics of Meaning* (Oxford: Blackwell, 1993); Kenan Malik, *The Meaning of Race: Race, History, and Culture in Western Society* (New York: Routledge, 1998); Charles Mills, *The Racial Contract* (Ithaca, N.Y.: Cornell University Press, 1998); and James W. St. G. Walker, *"Race," Rights and the Law in the Supreme Court of Canada* (Waterloo: Wilfrid Laurier University Press, 1997).

4

Blood Brothers, Consumers, or Citizens?

Three Models of Identity—Ethnic, Commercial, and Civic

Benjamin R. Barber

Holding together multicultural nations has become one of democracy's greatest challenges. Because only a few dozen of two hundred nation-states counts as monocultural, it is not just obviously multicultural countries, such as Canada, Nigeria, Switzerland, Belgium, and the United States, that must seek common identity in something other than race, religion, and culture but also nations such as France, the United Kingdom, and China. Democracy has itself offered a solution to the challenge of multiculturalism by emphasizing civic identity as an extension of democratic membership—that is, citizenship. Alexis de Tocqueville had warned that nations conceived in liberty might have a particularly troublesome time maintaining integral unity. He knew that religion, a great bond in traditional societies, could not be counted on in modern societies rooted in political will and constitutional artifice, and under pressure from both secularism and diversity.

In the United States *E pluribus unum* has been the boast, but Americans are neither very united nor very comfortable with diversity. The problem, in Tocqueville's terms, was one of finding a surrogate for religion—a secular bond or what Jean-Jacques Rousseau conceived as a "civil religion." America's civil religion was a matter of what Justice Hugo Black would later call "constitutional faith," what Jürgen Habermas more recently has labeled "*Verfassungspatriotismus*." Divided by private faith, by race and gender, by class and ethnic origins, by geography and economics, citizens of multicultural nations have been compelled to fashion an artificial civic faith, a faith in the commons, to make up for their absent common cultural heritage.

The feisty English emigrant Frances Wright wrote in 1820 about the new American man (first referred to as such by Crevecouer): "They are Americans who have complied with the constitutional regulations of the United States . . . . wed the principles of America's declaration to their hearts and render the duties of American citizens practically in their lives." To Ralph Waldo Emerson, America offered "new lands, new men, new thought," while Theodore Roosevelt insisted that to be an American was "a question of principle, of idealism, of character, not a matter of birthplace, of creed, or line of descent."

Civic identity has its uses, and in America, France, Switzerland, and many other multicultural nations, has won a victory for unity over what might otherwise have been hopelessly divisive forces of difference. But over the last one hundred years, and particularly over the last decade, the underlying conditions on which the efficacy of constitutional faith depend have been badly eroded. And today there are two powerful rivals for identity that have nearly eclipsed the vibrant identity of citizen. For as the robust civil society on which the development of civic faith and the identity of the citizen are based was gradually undermined, two rival identities emerged that have further corroded civic identity: a renewed tribalism that has underscored blood brotherhood and set tribe against tribe, culture against culture, people against people, in a kind of modern "Jihad," that is Balkanizing nation states throughout the world; and a postmodern commercial identity rooted in consumption that sees women and men as clients and consumers of economic, technological, and market forces that demand integration and uniformity and that are mesmerizing peopled everywhere with fast music, fast computers, and fast food—with MTV, MacIntosh, and McDonald's—pressing nations into one commercially homogenous global theme park, one "McWorld" tied together by communications, information, entertainment, and commerce.

What these two rival identities (explored at length in *Jihad versus McWorld*, Times Books, 1995) and the worlds they reflect have in common is a kind of anarchy: the absence of common will and that conscious and collective human control under the guidance of law that we call democracy. Neither the tribal warrior nor the grasping consumer recognizes the claims of civil society or democratic citizenship. Both are indifferent to civil liberty. The tribesmen of Jihad forge communities of blood rooted in exclusion and hatred, communities that slight democracy in favor of tyrannical paternalism or consensual tribalism. McWorld's consumers pursue global markets rooted in profit. Each identity in its own way offers unity, but at the expense of democracy. The question is whether there is a foundation for civic unity that does not eschew democracy and whether the more tenuous bonds of citizens can survive the pounding of blood brotherhood and global consumerism.

I want to focus here primarily on the consumerist identity both because tribalism is so obviously at odds with democracy that I hardly need to be argued that its triumph will put an end to civil society but also because liberal ideology has foisted on us the myth that free markets offer a viable form of civil society and that the liberty of markets is somehow associated with or perhaps even identical to democratic freedom. So that while most observers will agree that Jihad's tribal identities are insidious to liberty, many will believe that global markets are an ally of freedom. On the contrary, I will suggest here that though in the short term tribalism may play more havoc with democratic multicultural societies, in the long term McWorld presents the greater peril.

The myth of markets is the most influential myth of our times. Few seem willing to question the seeming logic that makes the locution *democratic markets* so natural an expression. Yet the consumer is not a citizen and markets are not sovereign entities that can do all the things a civil society do. Thanks to the myth of markets, a disastrous confusion exists today between the moderate and mostly well-founded claim that flexibility regulated markets remain the most efficient instruments of economic productivity and wealth accumulation, and the zany, overblown claim that naked, wholly unregulated markets are the sole means by which we can produce and distribute everything we care about, from durable goods to spiritual values, from capital development to social justice, from profitability to sustainable environments, from private wealth to the essential commonweal. This second claim has moved some people to insist that goods as diverse and obviously public as education, culture, penology, full employment, social welfare, and ecological survival be handed over to the profit sector for arbitration and disposal—as if consumers one by one, spending their dollars and yen in accord with private wants, could somehow miraculously produce common goods and a healthy civic climate or nurture an identity as comforting as the tribe.

Markets are simply not designed to do the things democratic civil societies do, and consumers will not and cannot promote civic virtue by pursuing private ends. Markets enjoin private rather than public modes of discourse, allowing us as consumers to speak via our currencies of consumption to producers of material goods but preventing us from speaking as citizens to one another about the social consequences of our private market choices. Markets advance individualistic rather than social goals, permitting us to say as consumers, one by one, "I want a new VCR" or "How about some new Nikes?" but not allowing us as citizens to reply together, "There is too much violence in the movies" or "This city needs more athletic programs for kids!" Markets preclude "we" thinking of any kind at all, for consumers speak only the language of "me."

Markets are also contractual rather than communitarian, which means they stroke our solitary egos but leave unsatisfied our yearning for community, offering durable goods and fleeting dreams but not a common identity or collective membership. The communitarian defects of markets open the way to more savage and undemocratic forms of community such as blood brother tribalism and the exclusive communities of Jihad. In pushing citizenship aside, markets invite tribalism in. Finally, markets give us the goods but not the lives we want; prosperity for some, but despair for many and dignity for none. The consumer has an identity, but it is an identity that satisfies neither the demands of brotherhood nor the imperatives of equality and liberty.

The rivals to civic identity—blood brotherhood and consumerism—reduce politics to an unhappy choice between the market's universal church and a retribalizing politics of particularism. In the confrontation between Jihad and McWorld, between global commerce and its clients and parochial ethnicity and its tribesmen, the virtues of the mediating democratic nation are lost. Neither the consumer nor the tribesman aspires to secure the civic virtues that are undermined by the denationalizing practices of both Jihad and McWorld; neither global markets nor blood communities service public goods or pursue equality and justice. Jihad pursues a bloody politics of identity, McWorld a bloodless economics of profit. Belonging by default to McWorld, everyone is a consumer; seeking a repository for identity; everyone belongs to some neotribal congeries defined by fanatic religious conviction or imagined blood ties. But no one is a citizen. And without citizens, how can there be democracy?

Is there then any hope today for constitutional faith? For a civic identity rooted in civil society? Why has the middle ground fallen away? Once upon a time, there was a vital middling choice. Though in eclipse today, the powerful imagery of civil society held the key to America's early democratic energy and civic activism, just as it animated revolutions against communist despotism in Eastern Europe and Russia a decade ago. For it is the great virtue of civil society that it shares with government a sense of publicity and a regard for the general good and the common weal, yet (unlike government) it makes no claims to exercise a monopoly on legitimate coercion. Rather, it is a voluntary and in this sense "private" realm devoted to public goods. Civil society remains the domain of church, family, and voluntary association; the domain whose middling terms can potentially mediate the state and private sectors and offer women and men a space for activity that is both voluntary and public, that unites the virtue of the private sector—liberty—with the virtue of the public sector, a concern for community, and the interests of the commonweal. It can thus give individuals a sense of identity that is not entirely abstract without inviting ties that are hierarchical or exclusivist—based on an alienation from a foreign "other."

Civil society yields not only identity but also liberty. Alexis de Tocqueville celebrated the *local* character of American liberty and thought that democracy could be sustained only through vigorous civic activity in the municipalities and neighborhoods. He would scarcely recognize America today, where our alternatives are restricted to government gargantuanism or private greed or ethnic particularism masquerading as multicultural identity, and where the main consequence of the most recent election seems to be supplanting of New Deal arrogance by market triumphalism.

Foreign admirers of America have learned lessons from it that it has ignored. How ironic that the United States should be recalled to its own founding vision of civil society and its guiding constitutional faith by dissidents abroad employ-ing the idea to resist totalitarianism. In Vaclav Havel's Czechoslovakia where it helped transform the nation and in Fang Lizhi's China where it is being currently cultivated, civil society has proved itself to be an ideal of civic solidarity that serves as a prelude to democracy without inspiring parochial or exclusivist bonds. It has been clear to those who live under tyranny that freedom has first to be won by citizens establishing their own public space; only afterward can it be secured by constitutions and law. Constitutional faith is thus more than just a surrogate for traditional forms of community: it is the seedbed of democrat and the situation cries out for a reclaiming of civic space. At the time of the American founding, our Committees of Correspondence played a role comparable to that of civic forum in Eastern Europe, creating space for civic action in the face of an unre-sponsive colonial government. American government today is neither colonial nor totalitarian, but it has outgrown and finally usurped the space of civil society.

How did it come to pass that a nation that prides itself on its democratic civic tradition lost touch with the civil society foundations that gave that tradition re-silience? How could so rich a political idea, drawing sustenance from John Locke, James Madison, Thomas Jefferson, and Alexis de Tocqueville get shunted aside, leaving Americans and their admirers with an unhappy choice between the alternatives of tribalism, bureaucratic welfare-statism, and privatistic individual-ism? This constricting choice leaves the politically alienated publicly homeless: equally uncomfortable with what it understands to be a rapacious and unsympa-thetic government that it confronts as a foreign body to be cut down to size and curtailed with supermajorities, constitutional amendments, and term limits; and a . fragmented and self-absorbed private sector that can satisfy the public's yearning for neither community nor civic ideals.

Without a civil society to nourish engaged citizens, politicians turn into "professionals" out of touch with their constituencies, while citizens are re-duced to their whining antagonists—either angry purveyors of a politics of fear in which local identity becomes a bastion against equality; or ungrateful clients of government services they readily consume without being willing to pay for. William Bennett's *Book of Virtues* tells many a salutatory moral tale, but the virtues it celebrates are not produced by either government or markets, and there is a danger that Americans will think that the act of buying the book somehow is tantamount to acquiring the virtues. The virtues Bennett extols be-long to families and citizens and are nurtured in the free space of civil society. Tribes will nourish brothers but not tolerant and participatory civic equals. Character can be a source of renewal, but if anyone thinks commercial mar-kets are likely to have any better success in instilling character than govern-ment, they have not spent any time with consumption-obsessed-shoppers cruising Thursday evening suburban malls. Nor have they thought much about how easily the yearning for family values and old-fashioned community virtue can be satisfied by ethnic warfare and religious fanaticism.

What exactly is the civil society that gives constitutional faith its power? How might it be reconstituted in a fashion that gives citizens and politicians alike a space in which to act which is neither governmental nor commercial? A civic dwelling place that is neither a city hall nor a shopping mall? Civil society is no mere abstraction. The best way to move toward a definition is to think about the actual domains people occupy as they go about their daily business when they are engaged in neither politics (voting, jury service, paying taxes) nor commerce (working, producing, shopping, consuming). Such daily business includes going to church or synagogue, doing volunteer work, participating in a voluntary or civic association, supporting a philanthropy, joining a fraternal organization, contributing to a charity, and assuming responsibility in a PTA, neighborhood watch, or a hospital fund-raising society.

When we engage in these activities, we occupy civic space and (whether we know it or not) help define citizenship as membership in civil society rather than just as voting. Trouble is, we seem not to know it. Not so long ago, following a lecture on citizenship and civil society, a chastised middle-aged woman raised her hand and said to the speaker, "You shame me, sir! Clearly, being a citizen in civil society is vitally important. But I have to tell you, what with my chairing the church bazaar committee, my service at the hospital, my assignment on the PTA, and now I've been elected head of my block association, well, you see, I just don't have time to be a citizen!"

What we call things counts. We need to understand our civic engagements not as private activities but nongovernmental public activities and to call the space we share for purposes other than shopping or voting "civil society." For civil society shares with the private sector the gift of liberty: it is voluntary and is constituted by freely associated individuals and groups; but, unlike the private sector, it aims at common ground and consensual (i.e., integrative and collaborative) modes of action. Civil society is thus public without being coercive, voluntary without being privatized.

It is in this civil domain that such traditional civic institutions as foundations, schools, churches, public interest groups, voluntary associations, civic groups, and social movements belong. One thinks of organizations such as American Health Decisions, the Industrial Areas Foundation (from Saul Alinsky to Ernie Cortez), the Oregon Health Parliament, the National Issues Forums of the Kettering Foundation, the Study Circles Movement, policy juries, and deliberative video town meetings (see James Fishkin's work, for example); one can point to other practical and ongoing experiments in deliberation and consensus building among citizens who—without regarding of themselves as constituting a government or public authority—come together around their common aspirations as well as their conflicting interests to establish the civic space that is civil society. The media, too, where they privilege their public responsibilities over their commercial ambitions, are better understood as part of civil society than of the private sector. Only when the free space that is civil society goes unrecognized are we forced to treat all civic activity as private activity no different than commerce. This is how certain traditional liberal constituencies concerned with the public environment, public safety rules, full employment, and other social goods lost their status as public interest entities and seemed to reappear as private sector "special interest groups" indistinguishable from for-profit corporations and private associations with far narrower interests.

Throughout the nineteenth century, in Tocqueville's 1830s America and afterward, American society was composed of not two but three sectors — governmental, private, and also civil society. In that era when (as Tocqueville observed) liberty was local and civic activity more prevalent, a modest governmental sphere and an unassuming private sector were overshadowed by an extensive civil society tied together by school, church, town, and voluntary association. The Federalist Constitution and later the Unionist Republican Party, however expansive they looked by the standards of eighteenth-century Whig liberals who deeply distrusted *all* government, were by today's benchmark studies in civic humility. Though opponents feared he would be a kind of monarch, George Washington in fact governed with an executive staff that numbered only in the dozens. And the states and the people to whom the Tenth Amendment of the Bill of Rights had left all powers not expressly delegated to the central government by the Constitution were the real theater for civic action throughout much of the century.

In this simpler time, individuals thought of themselves as citizens, and their groups were civil associations; citizens and associations together comprised civil society, and its virtues helped constitute a viable constitutional faith. Only after the Civil War did they begin rapidly to lose ground to forming capitalist corporations with an appetite for expansion and a tendency to monopoly. As such corporations, legitimized as "legal persons" and limited liability partnerships, supplanted voluntary association as the primary actors on the nongovernmental side, market forces began to press in on and encroach on and crush civil society. With markets expanding radically, government responded with an aggressive campaign on behalf of the public weal, but not one directly involving the public. In taking on the powers it needed to confront the corporations, government inadvertently took its own toll on civic society, encroaching on and crushing it from the state side. Squeezed between the warring sectors of the two expanding monopolies, state and corporate, civil society lost its preeminent place in American life. Sometime during the era marked by the two Roosevelts, it vanished and its civic denizens were compelled to find sanctuary under the feudal tutelage of either big government (their protectors and social servants) or the private sector, where schools, churches, and foundations were forced to assume the identity of corporations and aspire to be no more than special interest groups formed for the particularistic ends of their members. Whether those ends were, say, market profitability or national moral consciousness, was irrelevant since by definition all private associations necessarily had private ends.

We are left stranded by this melancholy history in an era where civil society in America and, increasingly, thanks to McWorld, elsewhere is in eclipse and where citizens have neither home for their civic institutions nor voice with which to speak. Be passively serviced (or passively exploited) by the massive, busybody, bureaucratic state where the word *citizen* has no resonance and the only relevant civic act is voting (which less than half the eligible electorate engage in); or be defined by history and blood, religion, and race, as a tribesmen whose identity can be secured only through the eradication of others; or finally sign onto the selfishness and radical individualism of the private sector where the word *citizen* has no resonance and the only relevant activity is consuming (which just about everybody engages in). Be a "citizen," and vote the public scoundrels out of public office and/or be a consumer and exercise your private rights on behalf of your private interests: those are the only remaining obligations of the much diminished office of citizen.

It is against this background that the resuscitation of the idea of civil society as a mediating third domain between the overgrown governmental and the metastasizing private sectors, and thus as a seedbed for the cultivation of citizenship and constitutional faith, becomes crucial. Critics of big government think that the only way to shrink it is to cede power and privilege to the private sector: devolution of power turns out to mean privatization. By the same token, critics of an overly privatized market sector believe that the only to regulate and contain corruptions of the private sector and the market economy is to expand government.

Civil society is in fact *the* domain of citizens and the arena in which constitutional faith is made possible: a mediating domain between private markets and big government. Interposed between the state and the market, it can contain an obtrusive government without ceding public goods to the private sphere, while at the same time it can dissipate the atmospherics of solitariness and greed that surround markets without suffocating in an overly energetic big government's exhaust fumes and without yielding to the seductive perils of identity politics. For *both* government *and* the private sector can be humbled a little by a growing civil society that absorbs some of the public aspirations of government, without casting off its liberal character as a noncoercive association of equals engaged in voluntary activity.

To re-create civil society on this prescription does not necessarily entail a novel civic architecture; rather, it means a reconceptualization and repositioning of institutions already in place. It proposes that schools, foundations, community movements, the media, and other civil associations reclaim their public voice and political legitimacy against those who would write them off as hypocritical special interests. It offers the abstract idea of a public voice a palpable geography somewhere other than in the atlas of government or the dictionary of tribes and thus represents a crucial starting place in answering the question posed at the outset of this essay. Finally, it suggests that through common work, civil society might emerge from the eclipse into which it was propelled by, first, the rapid growth of the private market sector in the 1880s and 1890s (when American corporate energy first exploded) and then by the mirror-image expansion of government as it tried to contain the growth of the gilded age's predatorily productive monopoly corporations (before World War I) — an expansion that was further augmented by government's attempt to offer social safety nets for and a contrapuntal balance to a Depression-damaged, corporation-dominated private sector in the period of the New Deal.

The task today in theory no less than in practice is then to reilluminate public space for a civil society in eclipse. Societies that depend for their unity on monocultural particularism or a rekindling of tribal fervor are likely to break into civil war (Yugoslavia) or forfeit their democracy. Societies that pretend that market liberty is the same thing as civic liberty and depend on consumers to do the work of citizens are likely to achieve not unity but a plastic homogeneity — and, as with tribalism, to give up democracy. Unless a third way can be found between private markets and coercive government, between anarchistic individualism and dogmatic tribal communitarianism, we seem fated to enter an era in which in the space where our public voice should be heard will be a raucous babble that leaves the civic souls of nations forever mute.

5

+

Two Concepts of Universality and the Problem of Cultural Relativism

CAROL C. GOULD

To deal with the existence of cultural practices that violate human rights or oppress women or minorities or, again, to deal with the problems of persistent poverty and disregard of basic needs in less developed countries, several philosophers have recently argued that we need to return to a universalist and essentialist conception of human beings, in place of the dominant views that emphasize differences in cultures, genders, and so forth. This universalism has been advanced in a particularly clear way recently by Martha Nussbaum and Amartya Sen, Nussbaum using it primarily to provide a way to criticize the oppression of women (e.g., in opportunities for work, dress, or even in regard to female genital mutilation), and Sen using a capabilities approach to human functioning to criticize the unequal treatment of women as well as the existence of widespread poverty and the lack of general levels of well-being in societies such as India. This universalist perspective can be found in their essays in *Women, Culture and Development*, edited by Nussbaum and Jonathan Glover, and in other works.

In this chapter, I will criticize this move to return to what I have previously called an abstractly universalist conception of human beings, which remains overtly essentialist in its willingness to specify a determinate list of human characteristics shared by all and only humans. Despite the many helpful nuances that Nussbaum has introduced to the effect that such universals are open-ended and subject to consensus and historical interpretation, I will suggest that this approach remains subject to the older critique that has been made of essentialist approaches by feminist theorists and theorists of race and class, especially concerning the historically and culturally biased inclinations of such lists and their basis in characteristics of dominant groups, whether they be male, or white, or class based. These criticisms are even more telling, I will argue, when such essentialist conceptions are put forward as a basis for development and for human rights, because they may rather easily import Western liberal conceptions of norms of development and rights under the guise of the universally human. Indeed, this can permit cultural relativists to object correctly that other cultures have very different conceptions of human characteristics and functioning and of the claims humans make on each other, and that these are systematically excluded by such universalist approaches.

In the second part of the chapter, I will contrast this essentialist understanding of universality with an alternative conception of concrete universality (like that I advanced in earlier work—my 1974 article "The Woman Question" and *Rethinking Democracy*), which I will argue can also make room for universalist norms like equal freedom and human rights.

ABSTRACT UNIVERSALITY,
HUMAN BEINGS, AND DEVELOPMENT

Martha Nussbaum, Amartya Sen, as well as Susan Okin and numerous other feminist theorists, have recently criticized the postmodernist emphasis on multicultural differences and its apparent lack of a basis for objecting to oppressive cultural practices. From the feminist side, practices common in certain cultures, such as clitorodectomy, polygamy, requiring rape victims to marry rapists, or wife battery as a penalty for committing adultery, have struck these theorists (rightly, I would say) as abhorrent and deeply oppressive to women. Given the commitment to women's equality, such practices cannot be tolerated on the grounds of respect for diverse cultures. Likewise, in the area of development, theorists such as Sen have argued for the need for common standards for assessing development and for establishing priorities among aspects of development—for example, the importance of the provision of adequate nutrition and health care. From this standpoint, cultural relativist views, which may even be critical of the concept of development itself insofar as it connotes a Western notion of modernization, or which recognize irresolvable diversity in standards of development, are held to be deeply inadequate.

Consider a few examples of these criticisms: In the context of a critique of the concept of group rights, Susan Moller Okin writes in *Is Multiculturalism Bad for Women?*:

> Most cultures are suffused with practices and ideologies concerning gender. Suppose, then, that a culture endorses and facilitates the control of men over women in

various ways (even if informally, in the private sphere of domestic life). Suppose, too, that there are fairly clear disparities of power between the sexes, such that the more powerful, male members are those who are generally in a position to determine and articulate the group's beliefs, practices, and interests. Under such conditions, group rights are potentially, and in many cases actually, antifeminist. They substantially limit the capacities of women and girls of that culture to live with human dignity equal to that of men and boys, and to live as freely chosen lives as they can.[1]

Because of this, Okin concludes that respect for cultural practices must be subordinated to the requirement of women's equality. Her objection, we might add, is primarily from the standpoint of liberal theory, suitably modified by feminist concerns, rather than from a concern with a universalist perspective of, say, human rights.

The objection to cultural practices oppressive to women has also been made from the standpoint of universality itself. Thus, Nussbaum provides some examples of views of which she is critical: an American economist who urges the preservation of traditional ways of life in a rural area of India by arguing that—in Nussbaum's words—"whereas we Westerners experience a sharp split between the values that prevail in the workplace and the values that prevail in the home, here, by contrast, there exist what the economist calls 'the embedded way of life'; the same values obtaining in both places. His example: just as in the home a menstruating woman is thought to pollute the kitchen and therefore may not enter it, so too in the workplace a menstruating woman is taken to pollute the loom and may not enter the room where looms are kept."[2] Another interesting example that she provides is that of a French anthropologist who "expresses regret that the introduction of smallpox vaccination to India by the British eradicated the cult of Sittala Devi, the goddess to whom one used to pray in order to avert smallpox."[3] Assuming that the anthropologist was actually bemoaning the vaccine (which is difficult to believe), this would indeed be a case of cultural relativism run wild. We might be prompted to ask, Would the residents of India feel this way? In any case, we will soon turn to the question of whether cases of this sort require Nussbaum's essentialist/universalist response—that is, Nussbaum's specific version of an appeal to universal characteristics and norms.

A third example of pernicious cultural practices is provided by Amartya Sen, who focuses especially on women's status in developing countries as part of an argument for working out standards or bases for assessing and comparing levels of development worldwide. In the positive freedom tradition, Sen articulates a conception of "freedom to achieve" as the basis of this standard and proposes to represent this idea in terms of capabilities to function in various ways, which in turn anchors his approach to justice (which he thinks involves aggregative considerations as well).[4] His leading example of pernicious cultural practices is the phenomenon of missing women, according to him more than forty-four million in China, thirty-seven million in India, and a total exceeding one hundred million worldwide.[5] Who are these missing women?

They are the women lost to morbidity and mortality, mainly in Asia and North Africa, by comparison with the ratio of women to men that reflects their biological advantage (as high as 1.05 to 1 in Europe and North America).[6] Sen observes that this severe relative inequality of women worldwide is unjust, and it leads him to criticize any culturally relativist perspective that shies away from bluntly saying so.

I propose to focus here especially on Nussbaum's alternative to a cultural relativist perspective. She draws on Sen's positive freedom account of capabilities in the treatment of development but synthesizes it with her own interests in an Aristotelian theory of the essential characteristics of human beings and their virtues or their good human functioning. The result is a challenging account of universality and of its relevance in the debates about development. It is a conception of universality that sharply differs from the more usual one in this context. Thus, universalistic perspectives are not new where development and intercultural comparisons are concerned. The standard one is in fact the appeal to universal human rights as a basis for criticizing unacceptable actions and practices in cultures worldwide. Numerous others and I have in fact appealed to these rights as a basis for cross-cultural critique. I propose to return to them later and reintroduce them in a different context of universality from Nussbaum's. But I am jumping ahead here. Let's look at her Aristotelian/essentialist version of universality and see how it fares as an alternative to the postmodernist or cultural relativist positions that she so roundly rejects. I will also mention in passing some of the other views in the discussion of universality and development, such as those of Sen or again of Benhabib, but the initial point of entry to this question of the interpretation of universality will be Nussbaum, and specifically her article "Human Capabilities, Female Human Beings" in the collection she coedited on *Women, Culture and Development.*

Our question may therefore be posed as follows: While it is clearly necessary to go beyond both the postmodernist and the cultural relativist emphasis on differences, is the move we need to make to a straightforward humanism or essentialism? Do we need a conception of universality in the Aristotelian tradition of the sort Nussbaum proposes? This is how she puts it in her article: "My proposal is frankly universalist and 'essentialist.' That is, it asks us to focus on what is common to all, rather than on differences (although, as we shall see, it does not neglect these), and to see some capabilities and functions as more central, more at the core of human life, than others."[7] In her brief account of "the most important functions and capabilities of the human being, in terms of which human life is defined," she puts the question this way: "The basic idea is that we ask ourselves, 'What are the characteristic activities of the human being? What does the human being do, characteristically, as such—and not, say, as a member of a particular group, or particular local community?'"[8] (In passing, we are reminded of Marx's question in the *Grundrisse*—does the human being exist as such apart from his or her community?[9])

Nussbaum bravely answers this question with a list of basic functions and capabilities that define the human form of life—from mortality, through the body with its needs for food, drink, shelter, sex, and mobility; again, the capacity for pleasure and pain; the cognitive capabilities of perceiving, imagining, and thinking; early infant development; practical reason; affiliation with other human beings; relatedness to other species and to nature; humor and play; to what she calls separateness (each of us feels our own pain, etc.) and so-called "strong separateness" (each life has its own peculiar context and surroundings and, as Heidegger put it, is in each case mine). This list represents what she calls the first threshold, a level of capability to function "beneath which a life will be so impoverished that it will not be human at all."

There are some obvious questions here, already raised by others: Is a developmentally stunted child or a profoundly malnourished child who cannot play not human? These characteristics cannot really be definitional or criterial for the human, for then one lacking some important sort of perception or mobility would not be human. Surely this would be too strong (what about Helen Keller?), and Nussbaum would have to clarify the interpretation of these functions to rule out this implication. But let us presume that she can.

The second threshold is the higher one, which she claims is the main concern of public policy (but, we might object here in passing, such policy must also be concerned with the basics)—namely, the level "beneath which those characteristic functions are available in such a reduced way that, though we may judge the form of life a human one, we will not think it a good human life."[10] For Nussbaum, "[W]e don't want societies to make their citizens capable of the bare minimum. My view holds, with Aristotle, that a good human arrangement is one 'in accordance with which anyone whatsoever might do well and live a flourishing life' (Aristotle, *Politics* VIII.I)."[11]

For those unfamiliar with the details of this article, this second threshold is specified by a list of ten basic capabilities to function at which societies should aim for their citizens. These range from being able to live to the end of a life of normal range, through having good health and being adequately nourished, having adequate shelter, and so forth (all, by the way, grouped as one point of the ten); to having pleasurable and not painful experiences; to being able to perceive, think, and reason (again, one number); to being able to have attachments to things and other persons; to being able to form a conception of the good; to being able to live for others, also with concern for nature; to being able to laugh and play (very important to Nussbaum, obviously; equal to food, clothing, shelter, and reproduction put together); to being able to live one's own life and nobody else's (whose else could I live? But she means having the possibility of free choice); and, finally, to being able to live one's own life in one's own surroundings and context, with free associations and personal property.[12] She sums up by saying, "My claim is that a life that lacks any one of these capabilities, no matter what else it has, will fall short of being a good human life. So it would be reasonable to take these things as a focus for concern, in assessing the quality of life in a country and asking about the role of public policy in meeting human needs."[13]

This is a very rich theory indeed, but too rich perhaps for those who may find this approach to be in fact deeply culturally relative (i.e., expressive of a Western, indeed U.S., late twentieth-century view). Of course, this objection does not yet amount to anything, but it gives us pause. Somehow, such lists or specifications of the essential, from Aristotle, to Locke, and Kant, (with rationality as central, but in different senses), or Rousseau, or in a different tradition Fichte (with freedom as central), to, in yet another tradition, Marx and Engels (with productive activity as central), to Nussbaum (whose list is fuller than most of these, but crucially highlights separateness and strong separateness), inevitably strike us as culturally biased in an important way, if not ideologically one-sided or distorted (and this is not even to speak of the gender, racial, or class perspectives often evident in such views). Why is this the case, and can it be remedied within these essentialist theories? Is the problem simply that we have not gotten our essential properties correct, or is there a difficulty with this very enterprise of the construction of a universal characterization of human beings?

Long ago (in 1974), in an article entitled "The Woman Question: Philosophy of Liberation and the Liberation of Philosophy," I argued that it is precisely the conception of what I called "abstract universality" at work here that is the source of the problem. (I will return to the question of whether Nussbaum herself employs such a conception shortly.) Such a criterion of universality, as we have already seen with Nussbaum, attempts to characterize what is common to all human beings or to all societies at all times and abstracts from differences between them; in this way, it does not attend to merely local or accidental aspects of the human or social. In the classical view, it studies the human qua human, or human nature as such. Furthermore, in strong versions of this essentialist position, the universal properties must also be necessary (i.e., those without which the individuals would not be members of the given class and therefore properties that make them the kinds of things they are). In this view in which differences are taken to be accidental, it would follow that, in considering the human, all historical and social differentiation drops out, and only those abstracted properties that remain invariant for all humans and in all societies count as essential. These characteristics are seen as fixed rather than as historically changing. In my use, the term *abstract* is contrasted with its opposite, *concrete,* where *concrete* denotes those properties that individuate human beings or societies or that differentiate them—that is, make them the particular individuals or societies they are.

Aside from the many well-known philosophical critiques that can be made of this position, (which was also a focus of my earlier article), the more practical criticism in this context is that the use of the criterion of abstract universality to determine essential human properties is apparently not a value-free, but a value-laden one, that it tends to reflect the interests, needs, and prejudices of particular social groups. (Moreover, the rank order of essential traits tends to be determined by the relative roles and priorities that these properties have in a given social system.) This is problematic especially because essentialism tends to mask the particular interests under the guise of universality and therefore is deceptive. On my view, it is the very abstractness of the criterion that in fact opens it to such distortion, by way of its exclusion of concrete social and historical differences as accidental and therefore philosophically irrelevant. In the earlier critique, I showed that various great philosophers chose those properties as universally human that either the philosophers themselves explicitly identified as male properties or were associated with roles and functions in which males predominated.[14]

In establishing global standards for conduct and development, it seems possible that contemporary essentialist theories may similarly be introducing local characteristics from a particular social context under the guise of transhistorical, necessary, and human ones. When one hears of strong separateness as a basic human good or play as a basic capability (a concept owing a great deal to Schiller and Freud and other relatively recent thinkers), one is forced to reflect on the apparently inevitable selectivity and perspectival character of such lists. This is not to say that Nussbaum is wrong about the importance of strong separateness or play, only to put in question the universality or essentiality of the list. We could ask why isn't it also characteristic of human beings to want love or security or to live in a community? These are presumably covered under other headings—love and community under affiliation, security under the need for shelter or early infant development (?) or property (?), but this raises the issue of the level and description of the characteristics. Why these and not others? Maybe we should add some negative capabilities that are characteristic capabilities of many, if not most, people—such as jealousy or selfishness or even violence. According to Jerry Springer, everyone is a voyeur. Why doesn't this count? Isn't the list in fact socially, historically, and culturally very deeply variable? And, as both Marxists and postmodernists would point out, such lists tend to miss the connection to power and the powerful in a given social context. If so, do not such attempts to characterize the human, particularly as a basis for public policy (and not just a relatively harmless philosophical theory), end up being coercive, to the degree that they impose the standards of one particular culture on others? This would be especially so in the area of development policy. Wouldn't it be better, we might suggest, to see both development and the self-understanding of the human from the other's point of view? Indeed, we might further ask, shouldn't development policy be decided democratically by each affected country or, at least, by equal participation of all countries? (Or, more radically, do we in fact need agreement on general standards of development that would apply to other countries?)

One more set of questions presents itself: Since the list seems to presuppose a rich philosophical theory concerning the human, is it plausible to suppose that agreement on the contents of such an articulated and controversial philosophical perspective is required to guide public policy? Isn't this just another case of philosophical hybris? If we need global agreement on universal principles or

guidelines, shouldn't they be kept a bit less voluminous, not necessarily mini-
mal, of course, but perhaps more open and clear? Nussbaum claims that the list
she offers is vague and therefore open, but it is in fact highly determinate and
from a fundamentally classical philosophical perspective.

Nussbaum is well aware of most of these and other criticisms of her view and
attempts to meet them in various ways. It would be helpful now to examine the
transformations in essentialism that she introduces to see whether they go far
enough or whether, as I shall suggest, a newer conception of universality is in fact
required. We will leave aside the transformations that are introduced by Nussbaum's interpretation of the universal characteristics in terms of a positive freedom conception of capabilities to function, which in her case is specifically derived from Sen's work. I believe this is a salutary move and share the view that a
conception of positive freedom is required. I have elaborated this in terms of a
conception of the development of capacities or self-development.[15]

More to the point here are the other qualifications that Nussbaum introduces to
make her view more nuanced and less open to the criticisms that it neglects historical and cultural differences, or that it tells people the choices they should
make and thus fails to respect their autonomy, or that it inevitably excludes the
powerless in its application. Importantly, Nussbaum suggests that "universal
ideas of the human do arise within history and from human experience, and they
can ground themselves in experience."[16] This sounds good to me, but what is its
cash value in her account? It turns out that it permits the specification or interpretation from diverse cultural perspectives of each of the items on Nussbaum's
lists, but she does not seem to think that the choice of which items should make
up the list is itself historically or culturally emergent. Thus, she writes, "The list
claims to have identified in a very general way components that are fundamental
to any human life. But it allows in its very design for the possibility of multiple
specifications of each of the components." She continues, "[T]he constitutive circumstances of human life, while broadly shared, are themselves realized in different forms in different societies."[17] There is the idea that we have a common
conversation concerning the interpretation of these basic capabilities. The second
threshold list—of good functioning—is even more open; it is subject to plural and
local specification. But, in this short article, at least, she seems to resist the idea
that there can be multiple fundamental conceptions of human functioning that
emerge and change historically, culturally, and socially. It seems problematic to
me, however, to propose that we can have a conversation on the interpretation of
the essential properties, but not on which properties are essential. If we suppose
that there is consensus on the list itself, which she may be suggesting (certainly
one finds this in Benhabib's version), then we may well have a case of bad faith,
since it turns out that the consensus is for clearly Western, late twentieth-century
views. (Voilà! We have a consensus, and it is precisely on what we believe!) If
the consensus is on a philosophical theory (rather than just a twentieth-century
outlook more loosely), then this seems rather an implausible claim. As I asked be-

fore, how will we get people worldwide to agree to a detailed and contestable philosophical position? If, on the other hand, Nussbaum rules out subjecting the choice of essential properties to consensus or the object of a "common conversation," as I believe she has done, then is this really an alternative type of essentialism at all? It would seem rather to be the older ahistorical essentialism again, with perhaps the gloss of an openness to the interpretation of the details of the theory in each cultural and historical context.

Nussbaum adequately addresses the objection that such a list would remove personal autonomy. She does this by invoking the positive freedom idea that the issue here is the government (or, perhaps better, society) providing people with the means or resources for acting as they choose, not by making choices for them. All well and good as far as the choices of individuals goes. But Nussbaum misses the more difficult objection that this essentialism at least in contexts of development may be coercive or imperialist relative to the collective choices of other societies or their divergent cultural interpretations. Even if these choices as to priorities of resources or courses of development are democratically made in these other societies or cultures, Nussbaum's view would seem to require us to reject them, if they are not in accordance with the lists.

Finally, to the important objection that conceptions of essential human properties exclude the powerless, Nussbaum rightly points to the role that the conception of the human has played in countering prejudice and exclusion over the long haul (we can hope so, anyway!). In response to the claim that the basic human capacity to develop various capabilities to function has frequently been denied to women, she says, "[I]f we examine the history of these denials we see, I believe, the great power of the conception of the human as a source of moral claims." Later in the same piece, she speaks of "the power of a universal conception of the human being in claims of justice for women."[18] As I similarly argued in the 1974 article, such universal norms do play an important role in revealing when an injustice has been done, simply by showing that some human being has not been treated equally. We can know that a violation of universality has occurred. But, I would propose, we will not know why or on what grounds. Knowing the sources of a case of injustice is required if one is concerned not only with rectifying the specific case, but with eliminating the conditions that give rise to the injustice in their first place. Thus, abstract norms permit us to deal with the effects of injustice, but not with its causes. An alternative conception of universality, in one of its aspects, may be superior in this regard.

CONCRETE UNIVERSALITY AND HUMAN RIGHTS

If we want to avoid cultural relativism but still wish to give due weight to the claims and strengths of other cultures, should we replace the conception of abstract universality and the norms based on it with another conception of universality? The answer, I think, is yes and no. I believe that two moves are required: one, the introduction of a conception of concrete universality, both as a characterization and as a norm; and second, a more refined and less philosophically demanding conception of an abstractly universal norm, such that it can be more fully cross-cultural and less biased. Ideally, we would also be able to show the relation of these two conceptions—namely, the abstract and the concrete—to each other and establish their mutual coherence. In this rather short frame, I wish to set out the parameters and basic characteristics of each of these, to suggest possible directions for future research.

Let me start with the more unusual notion of concrete universality. I am no longer entirely comfortable with one aspect of the characterization that I gave of this in "The Woman Question" article, where it is understood to arise from the totality of interrelations within a society. The conception of concrete universality in Hegel's use, and to some degree Marx's as well, regards society as made up of internal relations among individuals who are mutually interconstituting. However, if this is extended beyond a given society to a global context of interrelating individuals and societies, it would seem to pose a requirement for some sort of unity that is unimaginable and thus quite empty. Furthermore, in Marx if not in Hegel, there is little discussion of the universal norm or norms that might emerge from this description of society as a totality of interrelations, so the import of this interactive understanding of individuals, however attractive it may be, remains unclear in the value context.

It would be better, I think, to conceive of society as constructed by individuals in concrete and differentiated social relations, but where there is no presumption of totality, but only networks of relationships, themselves interconnecting (like the Internet, only less commercialized!). In a more global context of interacting cultures, we might suppose that diverse cultural groups contribute to an increasing interdependence, within shared and overlapping contexts at a given historical period. In one sense, this globalization is at the same time a universalization practically speaking, in that it is marked by increasing interconnection, certainly from economic and environmental standpoints, and to some extent from social or personal ones as well.[19] The idea of a shared world comes to have a global interpretation, where previously it may have had more local ones,[20] and in this way, perhaps, the notion of one world may have some place, not in a Hegelian sense of totality, of course, but rather only as a potential framework for interaction. In the context of globalization, individuals may also become more universalized and less localized, as Marx observed,[21] in becoming many-sided, subject to culturally and socially diverse influences and open to a wide variety of interactions in many spheres. This does not, however, necessitate a wholly cosmopolitan conception of the individual, for we may suppose that this person remains rooted in one or two cultures but is open to many of them and their influence.

From the analytical standpoint, a conception of concrete universality that emphasizes networks of social relationships is at least an important supplement to

any abstract characterization we might be able to give of all human beings. It suggests not that "affiliation" (to use Nussbaum's phrase) is simply one among many
other human traits but that social interaction frames all of them in profound ways.
Even basic bodily needs and functions take on their shape and significance within
social, historical, and cultural frameworks (e.g., "I need a slice of pizza" or "I
need a Ben & Jerry's ice cream cone"; my body, too, is partly experienced by me
as others perceive it; or in hugging my child I become part of him for the moment, etc.). This has by now become practically a truism in social philosophy, but
it requires that we characterize the human not only atomistically but socially as
well, where characteristics are not only interpreted but constructed through the
concrete interactions of particular caring and choosing individuals, who are often
concerned for each other and choose together with others.

What would this signify for the norm of universality? Should it too be thought
of as relationally constructed through the concrete interactions, contributions, and
communications of such historically situated individuals who would approach it
from different cultural perspectives? And what would this mean?

For our purposes in this chapter, conceiving of universal norms, values, or obligations as emerging from such an interaction of cultures or, better, of people in
diverse cultures, has much appeal. If true, it would allow us to claim, in bringing
to bear a universal norm, that we are respecting these cultures and not merely
privileging our own, but it also would not see the norms as simply relative to a
given cultural context. One version of this view might regard the values as emerging from a consensus or conversation that was fully open (not one constrained by
apparently modern Western views, as the idea of consensus in Nussbaum, Habermas, or Benhabib perhaps is). However, theorists are understandably reluctant to
go this way, since, without built-in liberal constraints, the results would probably
not be acceptable, or else no consensus could be achieved.

There is surely some truth to the view of the emergence of norms from interactive multicultural contexts or from communication across cultures, and this
goes part of the way toward the specification of a conception of concrete universality. Let us take the crucial conception of human rights itself, which is central
to our discussion here and so is particularly significant. Contrary to the idea that
it is simply a Western conception, the contemporary notion of the human rights is
distinctively pluricultural. We may leave aside the as yet rather undeveloped
claims that have been made to the effect that human rights, either as a general
conception or in regard to some specific rights, can be found in the Koran or in
Chinese or other texts, though some of these claims may have merit, even if they
seem to arise retrospectively, as a reconstruction of possible origins after the
fact.[22] More to the point, it can be noted that the content of the UN list of human
rights (in the Declaration and related documents) in fact reflects the conceptions
of developing countries as much as those of North America and Western Europe
in its extensive list of rights tied to basic needs, such as means of subsistence,
health care, employment, development, and so forth. As we know, the coalition

of Eastern Europe—with its Marxist views at the time—and the so-called third world countries ensured the adoption of a document that did not privilege Western liberal conceptions of the priority of liberty and security of the person, or private property and democratic forms of political participation.

But what of the concept of human rights itself? This seems much less multicultural in origin, obviously deriving from the modern Western rights tradition. Yet, if we wanted to see a cross-cultural aspect here, we could stress both the political interpretation of such human rights, where they more loosely refer to claims that societies can make on each other, as well as to the protection they give for oppressed individuals worldwide, and the fact that from their own diverse perspectives, a wide variety of countries in fact did sign on to them (although admittedly not necessarily as natural expressions of their own cultural perspectives). However, it might be more straightforward to say that the concept itself is in fact Western in origin, although it now appeals to people in various cultures, perhaps because of so-called "modernization" in these cultures, or because it provides a critical edge to those seeking progressive changes there.[23] After all, as Benhabib and others correctly point out, we must not underestimate the importance of evolution or debate within cultures worldwide, partly in reaction to external influences.[24] Yet, despite the Western framework of rights discourse itself, which conceives rights as inhering in individuals, the other aspect of rights—that they are claims or even demands we can make on each other and that they arise in a context of mutual recognition—is a more communitarian notion that goes beyond at least the liberal tradition in Western thought and certainly has resonances, if not also roots, in other cultural traditions.

Does it make sense, then, to speak of values or norms generally, as well as specifically universal ones, as emerging from concrete interactions or communications among individuals or among cultures? Leaving aside the "ought" from "is" issue, since my emphasis is rather on the social interactive context for norms, and without attempting to introduce a new theory of value here, we can identify several aspects to such value emergence. There are three to note here: values generated in relationships of care and concern; those posited through common choices or coagency, whether based on common goals or on shared needs or interests; and norms generated through consensus or a common conversation. Although talk or, more elegantly, communication permeates the first two (i.e., care and choices), I believe these are not reducible to communicative discourse but are more practical, lived features of our interaction itself.

Care and concern for others has been widely discussed by feminist philosophers and some others in the philosophical tradition as well. Relationships of care or concern—often but not always personal—give rise to particular values that people or sometimes things may have for us, as well as (on reflection) to the value of care itself. These caring relationships or those expressing concern for others permeate ordinary life, from love and family, to neighborhood, work, voluntary groups, clubs, and associations of all sorts, but they may also be extensible to possible others at some remove from us, as, for example, Virginia Held or Marilyn Friedman have argued. In this context, others may be present as potential objects of our care or concern, as beings with needs, or as individuals who stand in mutual emotional relations with us.

Coagency in the determination of common goals (i.e., common choices) is also a key practical source of value. Things are endowed with value not only through our individual efforts to pursue them but through jointly chosen ends. These common goals are best understood as ingredient in our jointly pursued activities—for example, at the workplace, or in leisure, or in explicitly cooperative ventures of an economic or political sort—rather than necessarily as a subject of deliberation, which often comes after the fact. Shared ends or goals are posited as values for us in our experience. Others, including those from distant cultures, may present themselves here as potential coactors or cocreators in common projects. This is not to say, however, that they bring the same interests and background to these projects; we may instead appreciate precisely the differences of these others.

Yet, shared goals may well reflect our particular interests or needs, and they may in this way be initially rather one-sided. Taking note of how they function in value creation points to the crucial role that critical reflection can play in revealing the perspectival or even in some cases prejudiced nature of these values. And this emphasis on critique of one-sided needs and interests, both as social critique in terms of the social conditions and institutions that may contribute to them and as self-criticism by individuals or groups, is an advantage, I think, of such a concrete understanding of value creation.[25] In this context, we can understand values as initially based in interests or needs, or given as the goals of specific activities and projects, and hence as in the first place, at least, arising from the point of view of particular groups of individuals.

Efforts to achieve consensus on generalizable interests or norms, as Habermas, for example, discusses it, may indeed be helpful here, though whether it will lead to universal agreement, even ideally, is questionable. Such consensus or communication about values does, however, represent the third source of the genesis of value in practical contexts. We are always talking about what is important, personally and politically, which often leads to provisional agreements about values and norms. Of course, this communication is frequently about our concerns and common projects (aspects 1 and 2 just enumerated), but it can also introduce values of its own, whether rationally considered or less so. Here, the other may appear to us as a possible interlocutor in the dialogue.

Each of these three practical contexts of the genesis of norms seems to imply some conception of universality. Yet it does so in all three cases as some sort of limit concept or imaginary projection to which we can at most approximate. In the first case—that of care or concern for particular others—ties, and perhaps even obligations, to all others appears either as a limit notion or by analogy to the empathy or concern we feel for those with whom we directly interact. Certainly, contemporary communications technologies make it possible for us to experience the suffering of famine victims in the Sudan, for example, as powerfully (perhaps more so!) than the suffering of some in the local neighborhood. More philosophically, we may say that although there are practical limits to our caring and concern for others, there is no inherent boundary to its extensibility to particular others worldwide. We can also learn to reason in an imaginative way (and this is the kind of reasoning that Hannah Arendt thought Kant described in his Third Critique) from our understanding of the feelings and needs of those about whom we are immediately concerned to the feelings and needs of everyone, such that we can bring these others close to us in imagination and understand matters from their perspective. Developing this line of thought might provide us with a concern-based justification of universal obligations, or at least of potential universal ties.

A similar sort of extension might be made for the second and third aspects of the practical contexts of value creation. Setting common goals, which we take to be values for us, can involve increasingly large contexts of cooperative activity. It is involved in the small, such as groups of friends deciding to do something together; to intermediate cases, such as goal setting for a firm; to the very large, such as planning by national governments or international organizations, whether economic or political. Alternatively, the extension can be by way of multicultural creation or the interaction or confrontation of diverse individual or cultural projects. This sort of universalizing of coagency is thus imaginable, though it is not clear how much of a role it has beyond the concept of a sort of horizon or limit. Certainly, where common goals are oriented to meeting needs, an extension to the needs of all (perhaps coming to our awareness through a confrontation with the needs of others) and measures to meet these more extensive needs may indeed be useful. Clearly, too, worldwide cooperation at a general level is increasingly relevant in ecological and economic contexts, as previously noted. Furthermore, a process of universalization at the level of reflection and critique can also provide a helpful corrective to the potentially one-sided concern that groups tend to have in the satisfaction of their own needs and interests and the distortion in their outlook that this may entail.

In the third case as well, that of consensus and communication as a source of norms, universalization is often thought to play a role both in assuring that everyone may enter into the dialogue and in the idea that norms to be adopted should be agreeable to all affected by them. This essentially democratic idea may indeed be ingredient in the speech situation, as I think it also is more generally in the structure of interaction, to the extent that anyone with a reasonable consideration can raise it (perhaps if they have unreasonable considerations, those would be relevant too!). This opens the possibility of cross-cultural and intercultural dialogue, if we are careful not to make the constraints on the communication too one-sidedly liberal.

In all three of these practical contexts for normative activity, then, we can observe that a norm or value of universality of a concrete sort plays some role.

These add to the descriptive sense of concrete universality introduced earlier, where people are understood as tied together through their interactions and as transforming themselves through their relations with others. Furthermore, an emergent universalization in practice can be seen in processes of cultural interchange and growing interdependence across cultures. Yet, this still leaves open a number of questions concerning these various senses of universality. For example, is universal relatedness good in itself or because of its contribution to freedom or some other value? To the degree that it entails increasing cooperation among cultures, it might be thought to be valuable as such, or perhaps it derives its value from its contribution to the self-development of individuals (as expanding the options for choice or possibilities for growth of capacities) or perhaps from its contribution to sounder ideas, and so forth. In addition, although universal norms or values are posited in our experience, their status beyond a horizon or imaginary limit in the three cases studied is unclear, as is the relation of the conceptions of universality to each other. Moreover, it remains a question whether we can speak of universality in these normative senses as itself changing historically and socially, though the descriptive sense of it clearly does.

The most difficult set of questions for our purposes, though, is different: Even if we can show that important universal norms, like the human rights, are cross-cultural in that they draw on the contributions of many cultures or else that they have arisen through a universalizing consensus, this would not establish any independent normative status for them, and they would still be culturally relative, but now relative to the totality of cultures that contributed to them. Although our account suggests the importance of self-criticism and social critique with respect to the genesis of such norms to make sure they are not one-sided or ideologically distorted, it does not yet indicate how these norms can be used critically with respect to cultural practices in one or another culture. In a related way, even if we emphasize the role of intercultural interaction in the genesis of norms, this still does not show how we can criticize oppressive practices within any given culture, except from the standpoint of others, or even of all the others.

These considerations show the need for a moment of abstract universality and, in particular, a conception of universal human rights that can be used normatively to criticize cultural practices that violate them, such as those centering around the oppression of women that I noted at the outset of this chapter. Such rights could then be understood as setting constraints on cultural practices, whether in our own society or elsewhere. As rights pertaining to all humans as such, the abstractly universal norm of the human rights makes a claim to be based on a universal feature or features of human beings themselves. But as we have seen from the critique of Nussbaum's conception, we need to avoid an overly rich and highly determinate list of such features, if we are to avoid falling into the trap of the essentialism of a fixed human nature or into the error of projecting our own late twentieth-century liberal culture into a general account of the human. How can we do this? We need a conception of human beings that supports their equality with respect to these rights and the idea that each should recognize all the others as bearers of these human rights.

As in my earlier book *Rethinking Democracy*, I would propose that the basis of a principle of equal and universal human rights can be found in the transformative power of human agents itself—that is, their very capacity for social and historical transformation, or what I call their equal agency. Given the pervasive phenomenon of such change and development by differentiated and related individuals through time, as in fact is pointed to by the descriptive concept of concrete universality, we can see that the capacity or power for such transformation and self-transformation is characteristic of social individuals in all cultures. It is, we might say, ingredient in their activity, as an activity of growth and development through time. I believe that this capacity of humans as agents, which is both constructive and operates socially, can be referred to in terms of the idea of freedom, yet in a sense beyond the standard liberal conception of simple free choice, taken apart from such contexts of social transformation and the self-development of people through time. (Free choice is in a sense a specification of this capacity.) As characteristic of each human being as an agent, this power requires recognition by all the others. This recognition is at the same time the acknowledgment of the equality of others with me in respect of having this capacity and, in this sense, of their equal freedom.

As I argued in *Rethinking Democracy*, this bare capacity or agency, which I there characterized as a capacity for self-development but which I am here describing a little more broadly, requires social and material conditions for it to become concretely realized. If all equally possess this capacity, and if it requires conditions, then recognizing someone as human entails recognizing their (prima facie) equal rights or equally valid claims to these conditions. These conditions, I have suggested in *Rethinking*, include negative ones of freedom from interference and from oppression but also positive or enabling material and social conditions, including means of subsistence, health care, as well as social recognition of various sorts, access to education, training, culture, and so forth. This grounds the human rights, including basic ones necessary for any action whatever and nonbasic ones, necessary for the fuller development of people. Here, the account comes fairly close to the positive freedom view of Sen and to some degree Nussbaum, in terms of the idea that concrete material and social conditions are needed for the development of capacities (in addition to the political protections of liberty and democracy). In this context, it seems to me reasonable to speak, as they do, of the need to come to some agreements concerning which of these conditions are most crucial, though given the varieties of contexts for development, I would like to see a more variable list than they provide. Indeed, we can add that since these conditions are conditions for the development of agency or human capacities, which vary among individuals, it follows that although there is a prima facie requirement for equal access to conditions, the actual conditions needed will vary among individuals, as well as among cultures.

The conception of equal agency as a moment of universality that I have proposed seems to me considerably less culturally relative than that of Nussbaum, since it avoids the interpretation of strong separateness that informs her view. It does aim to provide something of an independent ground for human rights in suggesting that there is a characteristic of human beings that people recognize and ought to recognize when they regard the other as human and that this entails a conception of valid claims that each human being can make on all the others. In focusing on the power of social and personal transformation itself (or agency) as characteristic of humans, it presents a general characterization, which might be thought to be an essential trait. But I would argue that this is distinguished from traditional essentialist views, including that of Nussbaum, in avoiding any idea of fixed human characteristics or traits, which could compose a list of any sort. It is largely the fixedness of the characteristics that renders essentialism problematic. In the view presented here, it is the power of change and self-change itself, without a content, that is seized on as a sufficient basis for the recognition of equality and universality that is required for an effective human rights principle. This conception of human rights can then provide a crucial ground (as in fact it does) for criticizing and challenging practices in any culture that violate them. This sort of universalistic conception is indispensable, I think, if we are to avoid cultural relativism.

We can see that this sense of universality is dependent in some ways on the other sense discussed—namely, concrete universality. This is so both because the actual conception of human rights may be supposed to have emerged from the contributions of various cultural perspectives, but more so because of the way it is founded in the constructive and interactive power of differentiated individuals in society. I have suggested that it is this concrete universality of individuals acting in relations that underlies the recognition of people as having this power or agency. We may in turn abstract the latter from the practical contexts of activity and use it as a basis for a critical principle, inasmuch as it comes to be embodied in the norm of universal human rights. The conception of concrete universality thus can make room for crucial abstract norms like equal freedom or human rights because it sees the emergent relations and interactions that it characterizes as based on the agency of social individuals who have equally valid claims to the recognition of this agency and therefore equal rights in this sense.

Only by taking such a new double-sided approach to universality can we avoid falling into the opposite traps of cultural relativism on the one hand and essentialism on the other. The conception of universality set forth here provides important and much needed support for a nonrelativist conception of human rights, which can set limits to what is normatively acceptable in any culture but which can also nonetheless see universality and to some extent these rights themselves as constructed from the contributions of different cultural perspectives. Only such a conception of rights can do the necessary critical work of arguing against existent repressive cultural practices as much as against violations of traditionally protected liberties or the lack of provision of adequate means of subsistence.

NOTES

1. Susan Moller Okin, *Is Multiculturalism Bad for Women?* (Princeton, N.J.: Princeton University Press, 1999), 12.

2. Martha Nussbaum, "Human Capabilities, Female Human Beings," in *Women, Culture and Development,* ed. M. Nussbaum and J. Glover (New York: Oxford University Press, 1995), 64.

3. Nussbaum, "Human Capabilities," 26.

4. See Amartya Sen, "Gender Inequality and Theories of Justice," in *Women, Culture and Development,* ed. Nussbaum and Glover, 266–67.

5. Sen, "Gender Inequality," 259.

6. Sen, "Gender Inequality," 259.

7. Nussbaum, "Human Capabilities," 63.

8. Nussbaum, "Human Capabilities," 72.

9. See Karl Marx, *Grundrisse* (New York: Vintage, 1973), 265.

10. Nussbaum, "Human Capabilities," 81.

11. Nussbaum, "Human Capabilities," 81.

12. Nussbaum, "Human Capabilities," 83–85.

13. Nussbaum, "Human Capabilities," 85.

14. See Carol C. Gould, "The Woman Question: Philosophy of Liberation and the Liberation of Philosophy," *The Philosophical Forum,* special issue on "Women and Philosophy," ed. Carol C. Gould and Marx W. Wartofsky, 5, nos. 1–2 (Fall–Winter 1973–74): especially 5–25.

15. Carol C. Gould, *Marx's Social Ontology* (Cambridge, Mass.: MIT Press, 1978), especially chap. 2, and *Rethinking Democracy* (Cambridge: Cambridge University Press, 1988), especially chap. 1.

16. Nussbaum, "Human Capabilities," 69.

17. Nussbaum, "Human Capabilities," 93.

18. Nussbaum, "Human Capabilities," 98.

19. Andrew Collier, "Marxism and Universalism: Group Interests or a Shared World?" in *International Justice and the Third World,* ed. R. Attfield and B. Wilkins (London: Routledge, 1992), 87.

20. Collier, "Marxism and Universalism," 84–88.

21. Marx, *Grundrisse,* 409–10.

22. Jack Donnelly, *Universal Human Rights in Theory and Practice* (Ithaca, N.Y.: Cornell University Press, 1989), chap. 3.

23. Seyla Benhabib, "Cultural Complexity, Moral Interdependence, and the Global Dialogical Community," in *Women, Culture and Development,* ed. Nussbaum and Glover.

24. Benhabib, "Cultural Complexity."

25. Gould, "The Woman Question," especially 25–30.

6

The French Republic and the Claims of Diversity

Catherine Audard

The goal of this chapter is to provide an argument in support of the claims of diversity. This is a fairly banal endeavor in the Anglo-American context, but in the French republican tradition, it is a very different story. To value diversity as such is perceived as a possible threat to national unity and to the values of equality and the neutrality of the state that, since the French Revolution, have been at the heart of what it means to be a French citizen and a democrat. French immigration policies, while having been fairly generous in the past, have always insisted on the need for newcomers to fully assimilate and to become part of an integrated whole, the "civic nation," and certainly not in a "hyphenated way." The very ideal of the *République* is based, one should not forget, on the model of the ancient Greek or Latin city-states (*politeia*), and its aim has been to resist as much as possible the dangers of social fragmentation and anomie inherent in modernity, and to advocate a strongly integrated society in the wake of the various crises of modernity, individualism, and the quest for differentiation being one among many. This is a extremely valuable ideal that should not be rejected too lightly.

I would like to try to explain the fears to which the term *multiculturalism* gives rise in France. It seems that the French conception of the neutrality of the state (the French notion of *laïcité* or secularism) makes it very difficult to accept or recognize and even to see any value in the present multiethnic nature of society. My aim is both to understand the deep reasons for such fears and to provide arguments in favor of a more liberal mode of civic integration that would nevertheless appeal to the French tradition and preserve its strong points. My view is that such a rich tradition can be successfully remodeled to cater to the new social and cultural realities of multiethnicity. But only an argument insisting on the needs and rights of the individual rather than on those of the community, and on the nonnormative nature of the state, has any chance of being listened to and accepted in the present French context. I sketch such an argument here based on a new enriched concept of citizenship and on diversity seen as a need, following W. Kymlicka's well-known argument (1995: 82–83), for the flourishing of moral individuality, a flourishing that would lead to a firmer allegiance to the values of democracy within a more "decent" society.[1]

HOW ILLIBERAL IS THE "ILLIBERAL" REPUBLIC?

One of the main criticisms addressed to the French conception of participatory democracy, on this side of the Atlantic, has been its alleged illiberalism and its rejection of the claims of diversity in an age where recognition of difference is seen as an essential ingredient of a good polity. Be they gender, ethnic, or cultural differences, the French model seems to reject any consideration or understanding for differences other than in socioeconomic status and political opinions and therefore to belong surprisingly to another age. The first thing to explore, then, is the validity of such a criticism. Does it withstand a more nuanced and qualified view of the nature and purposes of the *République*? What are the reasons for such illiberal attitudes?

The republican model of integration, through a common national culture, education, and so forth, is presently in deep crisis. The claims of diversity, the "right to difference," which were just beginning to be recognized in the 1980s, have been replaced by strident assimilationist policies on the left as well as on the right. Recent years have seen a rise of far right ideologies and political movements based on a rejection of the "other." Xenophobia directed toward second- and third-generation immigrants, who had by this time gained citizenship, is rampant, even when no "real" foreigners are to be found. A general fear of a loss of national identity is spreading in the face of European integration and of what is called "mondialization."[2] Fear of a more fragmented society is growing, and the inner cities, the *banlieues* in France, are seen as symptoms of all that has gone wrong in France in recent years. But far from opting for a resolute move toward a greater understanding and recognition of the immigrant, mostly Muslim, population, the general attitude is one of contempt for and rejection of Anglo-American style solutions: multiculturalism is held to be unacceptable on the grounds that it would lead to more disintegration and to a destruction of the nation and its common identity.

Let us start with some clarifications. *Multiculturalism* refers both to a fact—the coexistence of fundamentally different cultures, some of them very much in a minority and very disadvantaged, and of competing sets of values within the nation-state—and to a social policy—recognition of these minority cultures and an effort to make up for past discrimination in ways that go beyond mere toleration.[3] This policy is part of a broader expectation: that a democratic society should fully recognize the plurality of the conceptions of the Good that exist within it and try not to impose a single pattern of behavior on its people, and that the unity of the nation should not be bought at the expense of its heterogeneity. Recognition of minority cultures, then, seems to go together with democratization and recognition of other minority categories based on sexual orientation, disabilities, and so forth, and, most important, with recognition of women's rights. But, in fact, whether all these issues require the same arguments and strategies is highly questionable as it is unclear whether the terms *groups* and *cultures* can be aptly applied to women, gays, blacks, Asians, and others. What these sections of the population have possibly in common is their rejection as unfair of "color-blind" policies that pretend to treat everybody impartially in the abstract.

Claims for greater liberalization and democratization seem, then, to be tightly connected with multiculturalism—or such, at least, is the view of the critics of the Enlightenment project as embodied in the French republican ideals of formal equality and liberty. In that light, France appears to be significantly backward and illiberal. The first question to ask, then, about France is, What kind of multiculturalism is rejected? Does the term mean the same thing here as it does in France? The concept of "thick" multiculturalism has been used by Yael Tamir[4] to refer to a society containing both liberal and illiberal cultures that have to coexist and to reach an understanding, however limited and superficial, to avoid major conflicts and fragmentation, whereas "thin" multiculturalism would only cover different forms of liberal culture and thus allow in principle for an overlapping consensus in the Rawlsian sense.

The case of France, at first sight, seems to be an illustration of "thick" multiculturalism. This may be seen in the recent conflicting events surrounding the wearing of the *hidjab* (Islamic scarf) in state schools by young Muslim girls. First this practice has been prohibited in the name of the neutrality of the state schools system (*la laïcité*). It has subsequently been reluctantly authorized, only to be banned again. The rulings of the Conseil d'État have been so carefully phrased that there seems to be no firm official view, leaving the local boards of governors and schools administration responsible for giving or refusing the authorization, and thus creating confusion and uncertainty. Many young Muslim girls, at the moment, are still excluded from schools, and there is no alternative religious schooling system available for them.[5] What happened was that a limited incident in a few secondary schools was transformed into a national issue because it touched on the very sense of what it is to be French, on the basis of national identity.[6] Multiculturalism, from the French point of view, is equivalent to the abandonment of the main tenets of the republican egalitarian and assimilationist tradition that is so central to French identity, as we shall see later. The main question, then, is to see whether this tradition is illiberal by definition or whether, as I shall try to show there is room within it for changes.

Following Tamir's distinctions, one could give at least three different readings of the incident:

1. as a conflict between a tolerant state and an illiberal religious minority, seen as "fundamentalist"—this was the reading of those, in France, who advocated the interdiction of the wearing of the scarf in the name of the emancipation of women from illiberal Islamic laws;
2. as a conflict between an illiberal state and legitimate Muslim ways of life—this would be the favored culturalist reading, based on cultural and moral contextualism;[7]
3. as a conflict between two illiberal cultures—this would be the reading of the liberal critique of the French republican assimilationist policy.[8]

I will turn, now, to some explanations, keeping in mind that to interpret what occurred as mere anti-Islamic prejudice and racism is not satisfactory.

Immigration has, over two centuries of colonialism and wars in Europe, produced a multiethnic state in France in a distinctive sense; this situation should not be confused with the American or Canadian cases.[9] France is a country whose borders were still changing at the turn of the century and which, all through the second half of the nineteenth century, had been integrating new populations, each with different languages, Italian dialects in the case of the Duchies of Savoy and Provence, German in the case of Alsace and Lorraine, and so forth. It was a country that was integrating Polish and Italian miners before World War I, Eastern Jewish and Central European craftsmen between the wars, over one million French colonists and their Muslim partisans during the war in Algeria, the *harkis*, after 1962. Today it contains roughly three million immigrants without full citizenship living on its territory. It is said that one French citizen in four has one foreign grandparent. And still France does not see itself as a multicultural, multiethnic society in the way in which the United States and Canada see themselves and in which Britain has recently began to acknowledge itself.

One obvious obstacle encountered in the formation of a modern French nation-state has been, as can be expected, the diversity of regional origins. But another obstacle has been the role played by the Catholic Church since the time of the French Revolution in one way or another. In keeping with a long tradition of conflicts with the monarchy, which would take too long to explain here, the church has seen itself, with varying intensity, as the instrument of the unification of society around strictly Catholic values, of the creation of a "*Jerusalem terrestre*" and, consequently, as the only source of legitimate political power. Thus, the creation of a secular state has meant from the start a constant struggle against an alternative source of unity and legitimacy. Therefore, especially during its beginnings at the time of the Third Republic, but still now to a lesser degree, to be "neutral" has meant for the French republic its non-Catholic, nonreligious denomination. To counteract the church's social and political influence, it has become, in a sense, its mirror image, and secularism as *laïcité* can be read as a kind of "secular faith" (*foi laïque* is Ferdinand Buisson's expression), which could explain, but not excuse, its strong anti-Muslim stance.

Another dimension of the specific problems raised by cultural diversity in France lies in the fact that, as a nation (and here it is very similar to the United States), modern France is the result of a political project, the formation of a community based not on "blood" or descent or on residence but on citizenship as a reflective commitment—"the nation as a community of citizens."[10] This emancipatory project has been articulated most strongly by the French Revolution, but it has deeper roots, which I cannot explore here. What was most hated in the old regime, in the remains of the feudal system around 1789, were the many particular interpersonal bonds between people, the particular so-called rights and obligations that, on the one hand, constituted the fabric of the organic society and of solidarity but, on the other hand, were symbols of oppression and injustice. (See, for instance, during the prerevolutionary period, the impact of Beaumarchais's play *The Marriage of Figaro*, which epitomized the evils of the feudal system through the magnifying glass of the *droit de cuissage* or "right to rape," the right for his lordship to the use of Susanna's untouched body before her legitimate owner, her husband.) In fighting these traditional bonds, the language of equal rights and abstract universalism have led to the ideal of the *République une et universelle*, an ideal that is still very central to French identity. To be or to become French was not simply to enter a particular ethnic, linguistic group or nation but to become an actor in a wider drama, that of an emancipatory process whose goal it was to eventually lead to a federation of democratic and peaceful nations, to universal reconciliation, to the dissolution of all particularities and differentiations, seen as sources of conflicts, to the recognition of a kind of universal brotherhood or world citizenship. The French Revolution had had the privilege of being the prime mover in this process by freeing the people from their particular roots and bonds and by "re-creating" them as the abstract bearers of rights: no more a Breton or an Auvergnat, a Jew or a Protestant, but a French citizen with equal rights and dignity. To be French, therefore, carried with it special responsibilities, very similar to those carried by the American notion of citizenship, those of enlightening the rest of the world as to the benefits of free and equal citizenship, beyond all differences of race, ethnic origins, language, and religion. France had invented the notion of the "civic nation" and, as such, constituted one particular instance of the "universal Republic."

In the creation of the civic nation, the state has had the primary role. In France, the nation derives from the state, versus the usual move from the existence of a nation toward its recognition as an independent state. The state had a mission: that of creating a new type of human being, the citizen in Rousseauist terms, by contrast with the *sujet*.[11] No longer a particular individual, devoted to particular pursuits, he or she becomes a citizen devoted to the public good. But at the same stroke, he becomes a Frenchman, no longer an Alsatian, a Breton, or a Provençal, attached to parochial communities. It is this confusion between selfish interests and particular identities that was to sow the seeds of unease in the face of diversity. But this was the price to pay to foster a new sense of national unity. As Dominique Schnapper, among others, has shown in her book on French citizenship, this ambition has been successful. Far from being a disincarnate basis for membership in the new nation-state, citizenship has a content, derived from a proper "grand narrative" based on the French Revolution and the Declaration of Human Rights. It uniquely combines a political dimension, the allegiance to democratic ideals, with the very powerful attraction to a national tradition and a community that one can be proud of.

This is shown in the emphasis in the schools' curriculum on history as a very important subject matter. One learns how to become French through the study of history and literature; the great writers and figures of the past provide models both for how to think and write and for membership of the French nation. This explains the emphasis on general knowledge, *"culture générale,"* rather than on personal experience and questioning, because the latter would be likely to lead to diversity, heterogeneity, anarchy perhaps—in any case, to a challenge to the forces of unification. It says a lot about the ideology of emancipation according to the republic that the Founding Fathers of the school system, the most famous of whom was Jules Ferry, should be disciples of authoritarian Auguste Comte, not of liberal John Stuart Mill![12] This authoritarian tendency can lead to seeing the republic as a quasi-totalitarian entity, the enemy of individual freedom and development.

But this judgment should be qualified. Citizenship has been and still is a successful political instrument for integration in spite of its strong ideological content. To paraphrase Simone de Beauvoir, one is not born French—one becomes French. The birth of a democratic community and allegiance to it are made possible by a seemingly totalitarian ideology, where the individual seems to be crushed, when, in fact, it is his or her local parochial attachments that are dismissed.

The question, then, is this: Can these attitudes change in view of the present new social conditions, and can there be an allegiance based on a new recognition of these parochial attachments, in the sense indicated by Charles Taylor and "the politics of recognition"? In my view, the notion of the civic nation, mentioned earlier, provides the pivot that not only explains the rejection of multiculturalism but could also provide the ethical element for a recognition of the claims of diversity.[13] The very concept of a "civic nation" is, in principle, the opposite of the concept of nationalism, but in reality it is still not completely free from it, as we have just seen. Because of its intrinsically artificial character and the fragility that goes with it, a different form of nationalism had to be invented. Doubts about French identity come from the voluntary character of the national link, the fact that it supposes values and choices on the part of citizens, and not only reiteration and simple facts, as in the case of the German tradition based on *jus sanguinis*, in which the ascription of citizenship is based only on descent.[14]

Let us consider, first, the exact meaning of the "civic nation," of the republic as a community of citizens, united and integrated in spite of their different cultural origins. By contrast with the ethnic nation, the political project of the civic nation does not take political homogeneity to coincide with similar cultural origins: it is not "given" as a kind of natural phenomenon, a second nature, as it were, but it is the result of a voluntary and conscious allegiance. But this does not mean that the political superstructure is superimposed or, so to speak, forced upon a divided, fragmented civil society. The nation is not given as such by the past, culture, or tradition but is created at any given time by the tacit adhesion of the citizen to its political institutions and to its core values: the nation, as Ernest Renan famously said, is "a daily plebiscite." This is the best definition of the republic as a voluntary political creation. It is neither given nor imposed but results from an endlessly renewed social compact.

But such an abstract ideal needs a very firm cultural basis to allow the durability of the nation. There lies the deep, long-standing paradox of a universalist political project, whose embodiment in the French state is necessarily particular; (the same paradox was encountered in the communist project, that of an international movement with national embodiments). To create modern social ties as strong as traditional commonality, the French nation had to become a sort of brotherhood, to implement a new common culture that would change the minds, the emotions, and the allegiances of its people, and this new culture, because of its fragility, could not tolerate diversity. Consequently, cultural pluralism has been, from the start, deeply threatening for such a project. This is why, if France is effectively a multiethnic society, it cannot take the risk of becoming a multicultural society. It is the one common culture that keeps the nation together, not merely the language, the national character, and so forth. The state has the mission of keeping that common culture alive and protecting the nation, of assimilating any diversity into the one and indivisible republic, of transforming differentiated individuals into equal and similar citizens, of dissolving the remaining small local communities into the undifferentiated body politic. In the case of France, then, the nation derives from the state, not the other way round. This is the main factor to keep in mind.

We have, then, two possible readings of the myth of a universal republic. Either we can see the French model of integration as nationalist and illiberal, its real intent being, beyond the rhetoric of equality, to effectively "frenchify" its population, to impose on it not only one language but one single culture, one way of thinking, irrespective of its various distinct identities, and all this in the name of emancipation. We can even see it as wanting to create the conditions necessary for the exercise of a strong central political domination in line with the monarchical or imperial inheritance. From this point of view, it would be an instrument of internal and external colonization and imperialism. Or we can see it as an effective way of avoiding nationalism, because of the political, normatively neutral nature of the nation. The strong unity of the nation as a united community comes from its political institutions, not from its vision of a common good or from it being "one" single people. This is a very important feature that one should keep in mind before criticizing too strongly the republican ideal, especially when one thinks of the attempt at articulating a similar conception in contemporary Germany, that of Habermas's "constitutional patriotism" and its failure to win widespread acceptance, since the reunification of Germany and the rise of German nationalism in the 1990s. Maintaining a balance between universality and particularity is or could be one of the merits of this model as long as universality is attributed only to the political institutions of the state and not to the cultural tradition within which they have emerged. But such a challenge is extremely difficult to meet. My point here, more modestly, is to say that at least a possibility exists of using this ambiguity to open up another vision of the "civic nation," a polycentric one within which differentiated subnational communities could flourish.

There is no better place to see that than in the present attitudes toward immigration: the only acceptable immigrant is one who totally abandons his or her native culture for a new emancipatory French citizenship and assimilates; but at the same time, the fear of a loss of national identity has made it more difficult for such an assimilation to be successful in the present social and political conditions. This is a no-win situation, which is fairly new. The normative aspect of the "civic nation," embodied, for instance, in certain strident and intolerant conceptions of the laicity of state schools, has once again made it difficult to assimilate fully without renouncing one's own sense of self-identity, of dignity. The *République* is becoming more and more humiliating for those who resist its values or are incapable of absorbing them. In a somber verdict, Fahrad Khosrokhavar writes, "In the name of the universal, the Republican ideology is in fact excluding the disadvantaged minorities."[15] The French model, then, appears to have failed the people all the more blatantly for having promised so much, perhaps too much. My view is that this is possibly a temporary failure and that possibilities of moving on and becoming more welcoming to minorities have not all completely dried up.

MODERNIZING THE "CIVIC NATION"

The point that I want to make now is that it may be possible to reinterpret the ideal of the civic nation in such a way as to make it capable of recognizing diversity and of coming fully to terms with modernity. As Claude Nicolet, in his reference book *L'Idée républicaine en France*, writes, "France is the only country in Europe where the great turning point, the great intellectual, scientific and political revolutions accomplished by the Scottish Enlightenment, around the end of the XVIIIth century, which have given birth, indeed, to modernity, has never been fully admitted."[16] Unfortunately, "modernization" for the French republicans has become more and more identified with a loss of national identity, with having to absorb alien liberal values, both cultural and political, to undergo a process of Anglicization (even worse, Americanization!) that would destroy its very identity. But at the same time, new features of contemporary French society can no longer be denied. We see more demands for individual freedom, self-development, and self-assertion, for more transparency in politics and decision-making processes, more integrity in the public domain. This leads to a new "postmodern" situation described in John Rawls's latest book, *Political Liberalism,* as pluralism. Pluralism, he writes, is "the natural outcome of the activities of human reason under enduring free institutions. To see reasonable pluralism as a disaster is to see the exercise of reason under the conditions of freedom as a disaster."[17] I would like now to examine briefly three areas where this modernization could and should take place: the conceptions of freedom and individuality, the civic nation, and the benefits of citizenship.

My first point is that current views on individuality and freedom would have to be modified. If the ideal of the civic nation is to be the result of a voluntary personal commitment, what kind of political freedom must be recognized to make this commitment at all possible? The classical republican view, mostly inspired by Rousseau and still alive in the contemporary French political context, is familiar enough. What is gained from democratic equality is, for Rousseau, a heroic sense of one's own freedom and dignity; the people that were once subjected to a master, be it a benevolent and peaceful one, are now sovereign and freed from the infamy of servility. The prize conquered by equal rights of citizenship is the freedom to say no in the Cartesian sense: freedom of thought is paramount in order for the citizen to be capable of a reflective commitment to his or her political institutions. Rousseau's view is fairly extreme in the sense that it was hoped that the acquisition of sovereignty by the people would be enough to change human nature and, "out of a selfish and limited animal, to make a sociable and rational being." Moral individuality, at least in the *Discourses* and the *Social Contract*, seems then to be created by citizenship, and there can be no way back to a nonpolitical moral nature, as was still possible for Locke. The republic is the mother of virtue, the cure for private vices, and it is on the basis of civic virtues that the moral character of the individual can be established.

Rousseau gives us the well-known version of republicanism with probably the strongest contrast between the "good" of citizenship and the evils of the private man, between civil society and the Republic. There is no psychological continuity, no transformation from within because, for him, as for the Enlightenment in general, man as a progressive being is the product of experience and education, of the institutional context. The political institutions, the new context created by equal rights, will be enough to create this new moral individuality. The only explanation that he gives for the birth of a moral individuality where previously only interests and egoism ruled is of a metaphysical nature: the essence of man is freedom, and this sacred spark had been nearly extinguished. Now, "without freedom of the will, there is no morality in action" (*Social Contract*, I, 5). The moral commitment to democracy is, then, of a metaphysical and quasi-religious nature: it is the attachment to our rediscovered true essence that has long been hidden behind the monstrosities and deformities of social conventions, as was the case for the statue of Glaucus (*Second Discourse*). It is thus fascinating to find an echo of this passionate longing for a "true self" in contemporary secular France and in its justification of the state's role in educating the citizen.

Apparently a long way from this heroic vision of the citizen's moral commitment to democracy, we find the instrumental-utilitarian conception of the good polity. The polity is good if and only if it can be proved that the individual's welfare has been improved, even maximized. We can talk, here, of the "good in people" that is brought about by the good polity,[18] which implies that this good is not necessarily what the people themselves would have chosen. But next to this illiberal view of utilitarianism is the Mill version in which individual welfare includes self-determination and the development of virtues, personal and political. The utility principle is an overall guide: it points to both material and moral welfare. Mill made this clear in his defense of representative government as a means to allow the flourishing of a creative individuality and to protect this individuality from the tyranny of public opinion. The system of rights and liberties is instrumental in the creation of a new individual, free from fear and servility. This is an echo of Rousseau's credo, in the sense that freedom is not valued as an end in itself but as a means to personal flourishing. Along these lines, we could advocate the recognition of diversity in the name of moral individuality.

My second point is that the ideal of the civic nation is perhaps not as explicitly modeled on the past, on the organicist view of the Athenian city-state, as it seemed at first sight. Indeed, the historical reality is much more complex. Henry Michel, in 1901, views republican democracy as "the city of autonomous consciences," recognizing the primacy of freedom of conscience.[19] Jules Ferry, the father of the public school system in France, insisted that the republic stops where "conscience starts." The République has been influenced by liberals who evolved and became republicans after the 1830s and the July Monarchy.[20] There has always been, within the republican movement, a more liberal trend that has been influential in the field of education. There is not just one single path. In politics, as in education policy, republicans were divided between "religious" sectarian hard-liners, willing to enforce a republican catechism, and more moderate defenders of freedom of conscience, like Célestin Bouglé or Ferdinand Buisson.[21] For them, Condorcet, not Rousseau, was the reference in their rejection of any kind of "political religion." It would be very interesting, of course, to draw a comparison between Mill's views on the need for a "religion" to overcome the critical phase society was in, and, at the same time, the republican view on *laïcité*, even if circumstances were extremely different in the two countries. The conception of the free citizen of the République does not simply refer to a reflective and idealized freedom of thought, whereby the free use of reason leads to Truth, as the doctrine of *laïcité* would have it, but it incorporates another set of very different and more liberal views where the right to believe and to worship whatever you want in private is essential.

The consequences are very different for the understanding of the civic virtues: commitment to Truth in the former case, as illustrated by the Dreyfus affair, commitment to toleration of others and to the protection of a private sphere in the latter. But the two versions share, in the end, a similar goal: autonomy and the self-respect that goes with it—in other words, the moral standing implied by the possession of political power and the exercise of basic liberties and rights. I have tried, then, to show that the civic nation implies a range of freedoms necessary for a reflective allegiance to its political institutions that cannot be limited to positive freedom, the so-called "freedom to," but that recognize the primacy of freedom of conscience and hence the inevitability of diversity and individuality. The policy of *laïcisation* in the schools, the administration, and elsewhere, has aimed not only at assimilating the various cultural components of the larger society but also at providing the necessary protections for such a central form of freedom, even if it has not always been successful. The protection of freedom of conscience is the entry to a French version of multiculturalism, and that is where the argument should be most successful.

The other controversial issue, in the ideal of the civic nation, is freedom of conscience. It is obvious again that the moral stance of the republican ideal is fairly authoritarian. Nicolet has shown that, even for the Third Republic's most individualistic advocates, freedom of conscience did not mean leaving individuals to their own devices but guiding them through a common culture, a common education toward "the abolition, in the minds of each and all, of these eternal enemies: transcendence, revealed truths, selfish self-interests, etc., in short anything that distracts the citizen from a full commitment to the Republic."[22] Nicolet even recognizes that "Republicans have had great difficulties in separating the State from its metaphysical foundations." Pierre Rosanvallon insists, and I think that he is right, on the strange alliance, in the French Republic, between democracy and what he calls political rationalism, which is the sort of contempt for ordinary common sense and judgment that leads to a stringent elitism and distrust of universal suffrage.[23] Indeed, the French republic would seem to have much in common with Plato's republic. Or does it?

It would be interesting to compare the views on education to be found in Jules Ferry and John Stuart Mill as both were similarly democrats but weary of the "tyranny of public opinion"; they both favored government by the most enlightened part of the population. The difference, of course, lies in Mill's vibrant defense of individuality and self-development. But I think that, a century later, the education system in France, among other factors, has produced an awareness of the kind of individuality that Mill hoped for. Individualism is a fact, neither an ideal nor a disaster, the difficulty being that the republic has to invent a new vocabulary to deal with the fact that inert and uneducated masses have been transformed into a majority of self-conscious and autonomous citizens. Rationality is not the only value that they can reflectively accept; *reasonableness* would be a better term to describe the congruent conceptions of the good that one can expect to see flourishing in a free society. This raises the question of the role of the common good: is the republic in fact still governed by a common good and, therefore, under the dictate of the general will, irrespective of the divergent views of its citizens? Again, a distinction should be made here between what can roughly be called classical republicanism and civic humanism. As Rawls says, the former can fairly easily be reconciled with liberal values as it relies on the participation of individual citizens in the political process, but it does not demand the disappearance of individuality, whereas the latter assumes that the only acceptable conception of the good is that which teaches that man is a political animal who should dedicate his energies and abilities to the good of the city and disappear altogether as an individual being.[24]

If I turn now to the question of the common good, again there is a possibility of reinterpreting the civic nation in nonnormative terms. I am here following Tamir's suggestions when she develops her views on liberal nationalism and Kymlicka's useful reminder of the distinction between the nation-state and subnational communities, even if the latter tend to be called nationalities.[25] The civic nation can, first, be described in communitarian terms, if we see it as similar to any other ethnic community, based on an overlapping consensus of shared values, on a vision of a common good, even if these values are freedom and equality for all its citizens. This leads to the cynical reading mentioned earlier, which views the civic nation as another instrument of imperialism under the name of universalistic values. And the German nationalistic reaction expressed by Fichte (1807) was quite blatantly a refusal not so much of these universalistic values as of the French ambitions that they betrayed.

But another reading is suggested. If the consensus on shared values is not seen as what binds together the nation but rather the continuous existence of a de facto historical community with all its diversity, then acceptance of different minority cultures and conceptions of the good is possible. As Tamir says, "the national bond is not broken even in cases of extreme normative disagreements. Since the roots of unity in national communities are outside the normative sphere, they can accommodate normative diversity and, in this sense, be more pluralistic than groups held together by shared values."[26] We can expect a better integration and recognition of subnational minorities in the French republic if nationalism is not altogether denied in the name of universalistic values or in that of a single vision of the common good but is channeled toward political institutions and practices. I agree with Tamir when she sees the communitarian understanding of the nation, be it ethnic or civic, as the true basis for nationalism. A polycentric reading of the nation, by contrast, has two major advantages: it frees it from the abstractions of classical liberalism and republicanism that make it impossible for people from minority cultures to identify fully with the dominant culture; it counteracts the oppressive nature of monocultural groups, of one-nation, one-state types of nationalism. "Reiterative universalism,"[27] by contrast with monological universalism, would be Tamir's suggestive answer to the problem, in the hope that the nation's nonnormative nature would provide peaceful and tolerant coexistence between diverse not necessarily liberal subnational groups. But I am, of course, conscious that a more careful analysis of the public norms of the republic and of the rhetorics that accompany them is needed here.

The third point, in my discussion of a modernized republic, concerns its value for its members. Does it deliver what it promised? What are its benefits that would consolidate its members' allegiance? Access to citizenship has been synonymous with social mobility and the acquisition of a new moral standing. But too often the two have been separated, and the dignity and responsibility promised by the republicans have been abandoned for easier targets. An example of such a process has been that of the frenchification of the peasantry through the working of the education system and the teaching of the French language. Why, for instance, did the people of Alsace, at the turn of the century, feel so strongly attached to France even though both their cultural and ethnic identities and attachments were much more obviously German than French? One reason is probably that the equal citizenship granted to them by the republic gave them wider possibilities, opened up for them more opportunities, of learning, of social prospects, of employment, and so forth, than if they had remained one of the many provinces of the German Empire. The attractions of modern citizenship counted much more for the majority of the people than the protection of a second-rate ethnic identity in an authoritarian empire. The same could be said to a lesser extent of peasants from Brittany, Central France, and elsewhere, for whom assimilation through the acquisition of the French language has meant an enormous gain, if only from the point of view of social mobility and work prospects. The French state has been and still is an immensely powerful purveyor of employment. One should, then, never underestimate the attractions of assimilation when it means social mobility within the framework and constraints of citizenship.

But does this really make up for the loss of precious local identities and attachments in the name of access to a new social status? Moreover, does this make up for the inevitable loss of self-respect that accompanies such a process? One could quote here Julien Sorel's exemplary story of social climbing in the new postrevolutionary order and Stendhal's hero's disastrous destiny: the self-contempt experienced for one's provincial origins and the assimilation process it so vividly illustrates have repeated themselves very often. What has been distorted here is the idea of citizenship as possessing a newfound dignity. The French story has been more one of social mobility, social status acquired through citizenship than one of personal, moral development in the Millian sense. The republican model, inspired by Greek and Latin antiquity, loves to talk about civic virtues and the value of political participation as the source of moral dignity. But the reality is very different. The loss of parochial identities and the politics of assimilation have been a source of hidden humiliation and self-hatred. They have become a real source of resentment when the content of citizenship has become thinner, when the value of fundamental rights has been eroded, first in their socioeconomical value (access to education, employment, fair wages, etc.), then in their moral standing (self-respect, demands for recognition, etc.), as in the contemporary case of North African immigrants in France. We could add that when the identities of these minority groups are themselves more problematic, integration is made even more difficult. It is when the process of assimilation is forced upon the people without the recognition of the different forms of cultural diversity and the compensation of full citizenship that things go wrong. We should, by contrast, ask for differentiated processes of integration.

   This leads me to my concluding remarks. The root of the problem in the French context, lies, as we have seen, in the ambiguities in the conception of the nation-state, not in diversity as such. Therefore, the major issue seems to me to be one of the meaning of citizenship: does it serve only the need for the state to control and assimilate the people, or does it benefit the people as such? Has it as one central aim the defense of the individual's rights to security and fulfillment? This is the major ambiguity. For instance, in the conflict between republicans and "differentialists" in France, concerning the issue of the hidjab mentioned earlier, it is typical that no space has been available for voicing liberal arguments based on respect for a valuable minority culture and its significance for the development of the individual, such arguments being immediately dubbed "individualistic" or "multiculturalist." The debate centers instead on the unity of the nation and its possible split into many ethnic groups, and it invariably bypasses the individual's needs for recognition and moral development through cultural, religious, and so forth, membership. The truth of the matter is that the centralized state feels threatened by minority cultures and seeks to enforce their allegiance and their assimilation into the dominant culture in order for the nation to survive. What is at stake is the making of the French nation, of a French citizenry; therefore, the nationalistic purposes of assimilation and the formation of "good citizens" tend to override simple toleration and basic respect for individual rights, a fortiori recognition of minority cultures. Against that, we have to show that recognition of diversity is a moral need that springs from the very nature of moral identity and the self and that this has to be acknowledged in a new and richer concept of citizenship. This leads me to the last section of this essay. I would like now, beyond the limits of the French case, to present my wider thesis and show how to make a tighter connection between citizenship and moral individuality.

CITIZENSHIP AND MORAL INDIVIDUALITY

It is only through being a member of the state that the individual has objectivity, truth and ethical life.

—Hegel, *Philosophy of Right*, §258

The point that I want to make now is the opposite of Hegel's. The reinterpretation of the civic nation as furnishing the individual with a rich context for his or her moral development provides the best argument by which to oppose the Jacobin conception of citizenship and its refusal of the value of cultural diversity. The claims of diversity should be met because they can be seen as giving a firmer foundation to the citizens' commitments and allegiance to democratic values. Here we have an answer to one of the most powerful critiques of liberalism from the republican point of view—namely, that liberal democracies are weakened by their individualistic basis, as shown by their citizens' lack of participation and commitment. A feature of liberal democracies, by contrast with republican rhetorics, is both their appeal to the good of the individual as a basis for legitimization and as an alternative to coercion and, consequently, their vulnerability when faced not only with conflicts but with the simple task of surviving the lack of individual commitment and participation in democratic politics. In other words, it is the individualistic dimension of democratic authority, which Pettit and Hamlin have aptly referred to as "the principle of individual relevance,"[28] that makes it so vulnerable and, sometimes, indefensible. This is the principle that brings moral individuality into the justification and stabilization process of democratic institutions and practices in contrast to the appeal to authority, tradition, or sheer coercion. What kind of citizens, then, should the members of the political association be to secure its survival, if no coercion is to be exerted, beyond that of the law? Should they not be some kind of angels? What is the source of their commitment to democratic institutions, especially when, as Rousseau said, the general will may quite often go against their particular wills and their particular interests? Obviously the answers will differ according to the degree and kind of liberalism we are discussing.

My argument runs as follows. The obvious vulnerability of democracies to individual preferences noted by republicans can be overcome if these preferences are not mere whims but real moral commitments. Then, recognizing diversity as a basis for moral development will strengthen allegiance to democratic institutions. Multicultural citizenship, by contrast with monocultural citizenship, is valuable both for the individual, for the flourishing of his or her moral individuality and the securing of his or her self-respect and dignity, and for the republic as it strengthens the individual's attachment to democratic values at a time when no one conception of the good can any longer unite the nation.

Let us, first, put aside rapidly the essentialist argument in favor of diversity. As Carol Gould and Seyla Benhabib, in their discussion of Young's position, have shown,[29] multiculturalism and the recognition of difference do not necessarily mean that "groups" or "cultures" or "minorities" exist as unchangeable and fixed essences as the differentialist argument seems to imply. The evidence of anthropologists is very helpful here in teaching us about the fluidity and the permanent renegotiation of cultural identities. I shall not insist on that particular point. If we abandon essentialist multiculturalism, then, we could find it useful to rework Habermas's concept of a "decentered society," in which discourse ethics permeate not only civil society but also political institutions. There are enough convergent views on how to combine pluralism and universalism, drawing on Walzer's "reiterative universalism" or Tamir's "polycentric nationalism," on which I will not elaborate here. Let us just say that the differentialist argument fails when it relies on simplistic relativistic views.

What kind of alternative argument can we then offer? As we have seen, the civic nation could provide the context par excellence for the development of moral individuality, because it is free from the imposition of a shared common good and allows for the possibility of a personal search for the truth and the development of our dialogical competencies. This was one of the tenets of the Enlightenment project: the project of emancipation thanks to the free exercise of human reason. But it is a troubled and difficult process, whereas parochial local allegiances, in imposing a common good, conveniently limit both personal autonomy and anxieties. Moral individuality, according to Mill or Rawls, is possibly an obstacle to smooth integration as it means that we want to live our lives from within and, consequently, we ask to be free to question our beliefs. The kind of allegiance based on that type of individuality is, by essence, reflective, which communitarians tend to see as a dissolving and sterile attitude (an echo of Hegel's analysis, in the *Phenomenology of Spirit*,[30] of 'pure insight', analytical thought, or *Gedanke*). This individuality has been interpreted by Michael Sandel as that of a "disencumbered self," deprived of any constitutive attachments to its ends. Such an interpretation is mistaken in that autonomy does not mean the absence of given norms or constraints but the possibility of their critical appraisal, in contrast to heteronomy. When both Mill and Rawls, following Kant, insist on the ability to detach oneself from one's own beliefs and to act on principles rather than according to authority or group pressure, and on the fact that this is the hallmark of moral individuality and responsibility, they do not deny the existence of the given context of shared beliefs and understandings. They deny the *constitutive* character of these beliefs. This is crucial for the making of the civic nation. If beliefs were constitutive, it would make it impossible to create a political association respectful of both diversity and freedom. The only viable political unity would be one based on a homogeneous cultural, religious, linguistic reality—that of the "ethnic nation." The point made by liberal thinkers, as we have seen with Tamir's liberal nationalism, is that the nation-state, as a political association or community, is radically different from its subnational communities in that it is nonnormative. Rousseau had noticed this, going much further in maintaining that these communities constituted obstacles to both the unity of the 'good' polity and the emergence of moral individuality. They are based on constitutive beliefs in a common good; the civic nation is, by contrast, a community of free and equal citizens who do not necessarily share the same particular good even if they share a common history and "societal culture," a nuance that is here essential.

Now, the difficulty is that in stressing the legalistic and abstract definition of citizenship as equality of basic rights and freedoms, liberals seem to forget that citizenship also means membership in a community, albeit not a "natural" or given ethnic community but one that is a "chosen" community. In the case of Rousseau, the key to the understanding of the general will is the civic nation. The same is true of Mill's individualism when he shows that the sort of freedom and equality that matters exists only within the limits of one's own nationality. In the case of Rawls, this is, of course, much clearer in the second Rawls, in *Political Liberalism*. But, unfortunately, Rawls confuses his reader when he says that the citizen is the moral person in the Kantian sense. What he should have said is that the respect attracted by citizenship is partly respect for the citizen as a bearer of rights in the Kantian sense, partly for the citizen as member of a larger and just society that recognizes these rights and principles of justice within a historical tradition. Failing that, Rawls is placed in Habermas's extremely difficult situation, of having to defend an allegiance to democracy on the basis of a "constitutional patriotism" with no "mother country" (or, even worse, no *Vaterland*) to speak of.

We now see more clearly how and why citizenship cannot be separated from patriotism and how attachment to democracy is the attachment to a community, a history, a culture. In the same way, the concepts of respect, self-respect, and dignity have no real meaning until they relate to a social context of recognition and valuation, the sphere of "public reason" for Rawls, where we may exercise our dialogical competencies. The dignity of the citizen cannot be separated from pride in being the member of a nation, involving not only shared beliefs but also institutions (like those based on the U.S. Constitution, the French Declaration of the Rights of Man, the German Basic Law, etc.) and commonly respected practices. The self-respect the social conditions of which are secured by the principles of justice is, equally, inseparable from self-esteem, from the individuals' mutual recognition of their own worth within their own community of justification and meaning by reference to shared understandings.[31] The republican ideal of the civic nation, understood in pluralistic terms, allows for a diversity of goals and pursuits within a secure framework of rights and liberties and "provides a secure foundation for individual autonomy and self-identity."[32] In conclusion, we should say, then, that our moral individuality, understood in narrative terms, values cultural membership not as a constitutive good but, to use Kymlicka's expression, as "a meaningful context of choice."

I now turn to a notion of self-identity that would be rich enough to secure commitments and responsibilities toward the good polity in the long term without necessitating a common good. One weakness of the republican as well as of the Rawlsian view on citizenship concerns the moral and cultural identity of the individual. Charles Taylor[33] has shown the poverty of the Enlightenment notion of the Self compared with the rich Romantic vision of the person. What is lacking, then, is a notion of narrative identity which, as we have seen earlier, leads naturally to incorporating the historical dimension of citizenship instead of treating it as the enemy within. Narrative identity can mean that we can choose to identify with certain values, within a tradition and a context, making it our own through our narrative powers, but also modifying these identifications. We are not instant beings; we possess a kind of "sameness" through time that is not, of course, pure self-identity but that is neither total discontinuity nor atomization. As Ricoeur says,[34] we should distinguish between identity as *idem*, strict sameness, and identity as *ipse,* or selfhood. A narrative conception of personal identity, says Ricoeur, allows us to overcome the contradictions between concordances and discordances, identity and diversity in our character by moving from the level of the character itself to the level of the narratives of which it is part: "it is the identity in the story that makes the identity of the character." The possibility of articulating the many distinct events that make up a life into a narrative is central to moral individuality. This possibility rests on the existence of what MacIntyre calls the "idea of a tradition," which allows for "the unity of a human life" in a narrative mode.[35] Ricoeur, here, recognizes the affinities of his own position with that of MacIntyre; it would be interesting to explore further the relation between the two.

The constitution of the self is, of course, an extremely complex phenomenon in which the nature of the political environment plays a greater role than has often been suspected. The communitarian critique has been very helpful in pointing to a central weakness in a liberal justification for democracy: its conception of moral individuality and its understanding of the concept of self-respect. But, because it tends to put the emphasis on the 'good' of membership in smaller communities and to see citizenship at the level of a nation-state as an empty legalistic and abstract shell, it has been disappointing in the end. The main point in the understanding of self-respect as the basic component of our moral and political identity is that it transforms mere individuality into a moral concept and cultural identity into a moral requirement, and it gives a firm grounding to our attachment to democratic values in terms of not only social but also moral benefits.

To conclude on that point, the value of cultural membership, which has recently been emphasized by many different authors, could be the following, even for a republican.[36] Full membership in a cultural group determines the horizon of one's opportunities. It facilitates social relations and integration; it most importantly constitutes (or contributes to) one's identity. It gives value to our individual choices. It fashions our sense of worth in terms not only of our personal achievements but of a belonging that yields a stronger identification. It gives more meaning to our actions as part of a collective endeavor. It connects us with the wider society and transcends our limitations by fostering a sense of belonging to a historical "imagined" community in the sense of Benedict Anderson.[37]

Should there therefore be rights attached to cultural membership? If we can accept that an individualistic foundation for the justification and stability of democracy can be enriched and understood in narrative and not only in instrumental terms, if we can follow Kymlicka and Tamir and see cultural membership not as an obstacle but as a vector of liberal citizenship, it remains to be seen what sorts of rights and institutions best embody this recognition within the political realm itself. In other words, should they be specific rights of cultural membership, specific protections of the valuable context of choice that such membership represents, notwithstanding the reluctance of states to recognize its importance? How can the necessary legal and political space be created for the development of a moral individuality that is autonomous but not self-created ex nihilo?

Kymlicka is right to draw a central distinction between two very different forms of cultural rights: the case of multinational states, as in Canada, where the different "nations" all aim at keeping their separate identities (especially Quebec), and the case of polyethnic states (United States) that result from immigration and where the quest for inclusion and assimilation is much stronger. Consequently, if new rights should be added and if political life should be modified to accommodate them, three different types of rights should be granted in a differentiated manner. First, self-government rights and federalism could be the answer in the case of a multinational state, whereas polyethnic rights should be the answer in the second case to secure a transition between first-generation immigration and full integration. Polyethnic rights are rights of the individual to be granted legal protection and financial support and solidarity in the exercise of his or her religious, linguistic, and cultural practices, in the strengthening of the corresponding institutions as long as they are congruent with the principles of justice and with the overall law of the country. They are the answer to the demands of a narrative identity that could develop within the framework of the nation-state, without threatening its unity, and could even contribute to it in a positive way. Cultures are never-ending processes of invention and adaptation as are individual narratives; minority rights are there to shape and orient these complex processes, not to fossilize them. The third type, special representation rights, might, by contrast, be a threat to the unity of the nation, if they were given permanent status, but the case would be different if they remain open to constant renegotiation.

The failure, for the moment, of both the republican tradition and the liberal conception of justice to generate policies congenial to cultural diversity should not be seen as final. If we look at the historical process that leads from the Declaration of the Rights of Man and the Citizen, in 1789, through the 1848

Revolution in France, to the recognition of the economic and social rights of the worker in the 1948 Universal Declaration, there is no reason why new rights should not be added to the list, allowing for new social and historical conditions to be taken into account. Rights being both the condition and the result of political "empowerment," we cannot expect that the process will be struggle-free. A first stage before new rights are identified and enacted is that of the socioeconomic struggle. The quest for inclusion is, first, the search for better living conditions; this is where attachments and commitments to democracy are first created and where new bonds are forged. Integration through citizenship has been a powerful vector of social mobility and modernization in the case of France. In that sense, previous rights, to employment, education, culture, and knowledge can be given a new meaning and might open the way to the fulfillment of the needs of moral individuality.

CONCLUSION

For the time being, French legislation has been unable to recognize the need for the protection of minority cultures and the usefulness of such rights to strengthen the attachment of minorities to the republic. In Rousseauist terms, any diversity is still seen as a threat to the unity of the nation. But, one could ask, if that was the case at the time of the French Revolution, after two centuries of strong state intervention, is the national identity still in danger of being overwhelmed by new waves of immigration? Obviously, the reasons that there is such a reluctance are very diverse and not necessarily acceptable. But, even if a compromise could be found, even if immigrant children of non-Christian origins were provided with the kind of education that they needed to become "good" French citizens and yet to keep in touch with their traditions if they wished to, as has been the case with all previous immigrations of Christian or Jewish origins, distinctions should be made within the sphere of minority or group-differentiated rights: they should always be rights of the individual, and they should be conducive to integration in the long run, not a source of division and hostility. This is why the process cannot be hastened and existing rights should be used to their whole potential, while the argument of the needs of moral individuality presented here should be emphasized, rather than the differentialist argument.

The task of political philosophy is to provide arguments and to make conceptual distinctions, where previous confusions could hamper appropriate policies or courses of action. It has, therefore, a strong normative dimension. Here, we have examined the ways in which a defense of democratic institutions, of the republic as a well-ordered society in the sense of Rawls, could be enriched by a narrative conception of moral individuality that allows for both the autonomy and the dialogical dimensions of personal development. This is not an easy position. Communitarian and culturalist/feminist critiques of both liberalism and republicanism are very attractive as they echo the demands of subnational communities to be respected and the claim that the unity of the larger society is a destructive myth, that we should reconcile ourselves to the conflictual nature of so many human ends in the sense of Isaiah Berlin's value pluralism. Still, the task remains of reconciling diversity and freedom, and the argument based on the needs of moral individuality seems a powerful one.

NOTES

1. Avishai Margalit, *The Decent Society* (Cambridge, Mass.: Harvard University Press, 1996). A decent society does not humiliate its most disadvantaged members in denying them any recognition of their most cherished traditions and beliefs.

2. Rogers Brubaker, *Citizenship and Nationhood in France and Germany* (Cambridge, Mass.: Harvard University Press, 1992), 187–89.

3. See Charles Taylor in *Multiculturalism,* ed. A. Gutmann (Princeton, N.J.: Princeton University Press 1994), 38.

4. Yael Tamir, "Two Concepts of Multiculturalism," *Journal of Philosophy of Education* 29, no. 2 (1995): 161–72.

5. See, among others, A. E. Galeotti "Citizenship and Equality: The Place for Toleration" *Political Theory* 21, no. 4 (1993): 585–605; "A Problem with Headscarves" *Political Theory* 22, no. 4 (1994): 653–72, for a detailed account of the events and their political significance. See also Tariq Modood, "Ethnic Difference and Racial Equality" in *Reinventing the Left*, ed. D. Millband (Cambridge, Mass.: Polity, 1994).

6. Similar conflicts erupted across Europe at the same time, but nowhere did they create difficulties and opposition on the same scale. In Britain, for instance, the importance of integrating young Muslim girls has been seen as paramount by most local education authorities, and one pragmatic answer was to allow the hidjab as long as it had the school uniform's colors. This is not to say that there are no difficulties, but they do not carry the same political and ideological weight.

7. Iris Marion Young, *Justice and the Politics of Difference* (Princeton, N.J.: Princeton University Press, 1990).

8. Modood, *Reinventing the Left*.

9. See, for useful comparisons, Will Kymlicka, *Multicultural Citizenship* (Oxford: Oxford University Press, 1995), 11–26.

10. Dominique Schnapper, *La Communauté des citoyens* (Paris: Gallimard, 1994).

11. J. J. Rousseau, *On Social Contract* (London: Penguin, 1967; originally published 1762), I: chap. 6.

12. Blandine Kriegel, "Liberté de conscience et citoyenneté" in *L'Identité française*, ed. F. Castro (Paris: Editions Tierce, 1985), 84, and the reference book on the question by Claude Nicolet, *L'Idée républicaine en France* (Paris: Gallimard, 1982).

13. Yael Tamir, *Liberal Nationalism* (Princeton, N.J.: Princeton University Press, 1993). As I will show later, my position would be close to that expressed by Tamir when she says that "the non-normative content of the nation allows the development and the flourishing of numerous normative, sub-national communities of identification" (90). In other words, the "civic nation" does not necessarily have to be homogeneous and assimilationist.

14. France and Germany differ from Britain and the United States in the sense that citizenship is ascribed to children of citizens, following *jus sanguinis*. But they differ between them in that French law automatically transforms second-generation immigrants into French citizens, incorporating some elements of *jus soli* or place of birth and residency; it is even the most common way to become French. Changing the law to bar certain categories of immigrants from becoming French would then make it impossible for children of French citizens to become French! See Brubaker, *Citizenship and Nationhood,* chaps. 4 and 7.

15. F. Khoroskhavar, "L'Universel abstrait, le politique et la construction de l'islamisme comme forme d'altérité," in *Une Société fragmentée: Le Multiculturalisme en débat,* ed. M. Wieviorka (Paris: La Découverte, 1996).

16. Nicolet, *L'Idée républicaine,* 479.

17. John Rawls, *Political Liberalism* (New York: Columbia University Press, 1993), xvi.

18. Alan Hamlin and Philip Pettit, eds., *The Good Polity* (Oxford: Blackwell, 1989), 8.

19. Henry Michel, in Nicolet, *L'Idée républicaine,* 483.

20. See Lucien Jaume's recent book, *L'Individu effacé* (Paris: Fayard, 1997), for a comprehensive history of the French liberals. See also S. Hazareesingh, *From Subject to Citizen* (1998).

21. Célestin Bouglé, *Pour la Liberté de conscience* (Paris: 1906), and Ferdinand Buisson, *La Foi laïque* (Paris: 1912).

22. Nicolet, *L'Idée républicaine,* 498.

23. Pierre Rosanvallon, *Le Sacre du citoyen* (Paris: Gallimard, 1992), 452.

24. Rawls, *Political Liberalism,* 206.

25. See Tamir, *Liberal Nationalism,* 6, and Kymlicka, *Multicultural Citizenship,* 92–93.

26. Tamir, *Liberal Nationalism,* 90.

27. Michael Walzer, *Spheres of Justice* (Oxford: Robertson, 1983), 86.

28. Hamlin and Pettit, *The Good Polity,* 8.

29. S. Benhabib, ed., *Democracy and Difference* (Princeton, N.J.: Princeton University Press, 1996).

30. G. F. Hegel, *Phenomenology of Spirit,* trans. A. V. Miller (Oxford: Oxford University Press, 1977), 547, 332.

31. David Sacks, "How to Distinguish Self-respect from Self-esteem," *Philosophy and Public Affairs* 10, no. 4 (1981).

32. Kymlicka, *Multicultural Citizenship,* 105.

33. Charles Taylor, *Sources of the Self* (Cambridge, Mass.: Harvard University Press, 1989).

34. P. Ricoeur, *Soi-même comme un autre* (Paris: Le Seuil, 1990), 140, 175, 180–88.

35. A. MacIntyre, *After Virtue* (London: Duckworth, 1981), chap. 15.

36. Joseph Raz, *Ethics in the Public Domain* (Oxford: Clarendon, 1994), 177; see also Kymlicka, *Multicultural Citizenship;* Tamir, *Liberal Nationalism;* and Axel Honneth, *The Struggle for Recognition* (Cambridge, Mass.: Polity, 1995), on the value of cultural membership.

37. B. Anderson, *Imagined Communities* (London: Verso, 1983).

REFERENCES

Anderson, Benedict. *Imagined Communities*. London: Verso, 1983.

Benhabib, Sheila, ed. *Democracy and Difference*. Princeton, N.J.: Princeton University Press, 1996.

Bouglé, Célestin. *Pour la Liberté de conscience*. Paris: 1906.

Brubaker, Rogers. *Citizenship and Nationhood in France and Germany*. Cambridge, Mass.: Harvard University Press, 1992.

Buisson, Ferdinand. *La Foi laïque*. Paris: 1912.

Galeotti, A. E. "Citizenship and Equality: The Place for Toleration." *Political Theory* 21, no. 4 (1993): 585–605.

Habermas, Jürgen. *Moral Consciousness and Communicative Action*. Cambridge, Mass.: MIT Press, 1990.

Hamlin, Alan, and Philip Pettit, eds. *The Good Polity*. Oxford: Blackwell, 1989.

Hazareesingh, Sudhir. *From Subject to Citizen*. Princeton, N.J.: Princeton University Press, 1998.

Hegel, G. F. *Phenomenology of Spirit*, trans. A. V. Miller. Oxford: Oxford University Press, 1977.

Honneth, Axel. *The Struggle for Recognition*. Cambridge, Mass.: Polity, 1995.

Jaume, Lucien. *L'Individu effacé*. Paris: Fayard, 1997.

Khoroskhavar, F. "L'Universel abstrait, le politique et la construction de l'islamisme comme forme d'altérité." In *Une Société fragmentée: Le Multiculturalisme en débat*, ed. M. Wieviorka. Paris: La Découverte, 1996.

Kriegel, Blandine. "Liberté de conscience et citoyenneté." In *L'Identité française*, ed. F. Castro Paris: Editions Tierce, 1985.

Kymlicka, Will. *Multicultural Citizenship*. Oxford: Oxford University Press, 1995.

Macintyre, Alistair. *After Virtue*. London: Duckworth, 1981.

Margalit, Avishai. *The Decent Society*. Cambridge, Mass.: Harvard University Press, 1996.

Modood, Tariq. "Ethnic Difference and Racial Equality." In *Reinventing the Left*, ed. D. Millband. Cambridge, Mass.: Polity, 1994.

Moruzzi, N. C. "A Problem with Headscarves." *Political Theory* 22, no. 4 (1994).

Nicolet, Claude. *L'Idée républicaine en France*. Paris: Gallimard, 1982.

Rawls, John. *Political Liberalism*. New York: Columbia University Press, 1993.

Raz, Joseph. *Ethics in the Public Domain*. Oxford: Clarendon, 1994.

Ricoeur, Paul. *Soi-même comme un autre*. Paris: Le Seuil, 1990.

Rosanvallon, Pierre. *Le Sacre du citoyen*. Paris: Gallimard, 1992.

Rousseau, Jean-Jacques. *On Social Contract*. London: Penguin, 1967 (originally published 1762).

Sacks, David. "How to Distinguish Self-respect from Self-esteem." *Philosophy and Public Affairs* 10, no. 4 (1981).

Sandel, Michael. *Liberalism and the Limits of Justice*. Cambridge: Cambridge University Press, 1982.

Schnapper, Dominique. *La Communauté des citoyens*. Paris: Gallimard, 1994.

Tamir, Yael. "Two Concepts of Multiculturalism." *Journal of Philosophy of Education* 29, no. 2 (1995): 161-72.

———. *Liberal Nationalism*. Princeton, N.J.: Princeton University Press, 1993.
Taylor, Charles. "Politics of recognition." In *Multiculturalism*, ed. A. Gutmann. Princeton, N.J.: Princeton University Press, 1994.
———. *Sources of the Self*. Cambridge, Mass.: Harvard University Press, 1989.
Walzer, Michael. *Spheres of Justice*. Oxford: Robertson, 1983.
Young, Iris Marion. *Justice and the Politics of Difference*. Princeton, N.J.: Princeton University Press, 1990.

7

Value Judgments and Political Assessments about National Models of Citizenship

The U.S. and French Cases

JAMES A. COHEN

MODELS OF CITIZENSHIP AND TERMS OF COMPARISON

The term *citizenship* refers in one way or another to state-sanctioned membership in a national society. Studies of citizenship can focus on several different aspects of such inclusion. In its most frequent usages, the term refers to the legal criteria used to determine membership or to the rights and obligations it entails. In recent years, however, studies of citizenship have come to focus more and more on modes of integration among individuals and groups of different ethnic and national origins, religious beliefs, genders, and sexual orientations. Citizenship refers here to the political logic at work in the management of diversity— that is, to the modes of recognition or nonrecognition of distinct identities within the broader fabric of a national mode of cohesion, when indeed such cohesion holds true. (At a time when ethnic nationalisms are provoking violent conflict in many areas of the world, it cannot be forgotten that certain societies, those of the "North," have achieved systems of socioeconomic and political integration that are privileged to have displayed a relative efficacy, whatever troubles they, too, might experience.)

Through comparative analysis it is possible to distinguish different national types or models of citizenship, whether reference be made to citizenship as legal status, citizenship as a set of rights, or citizenship as a mode of integration. My concern here is with the latter sense of the term. Models of integration of diversity are tightly bound up with broader models of national cohesion, but they also have logics of their own that merit exploration.

It is evident to anyone who has attempted, casually or more methodically, to compare two or more national societies that different modes of integration are at work. This chapter explores the comparison between the United States and France. While the models of citizenship of these two countries are grounded in similar philosophical ideals of democratic toleration and republican government, they are also different in fundamental ways, and this is clearly the case regarding their modes of managing ethnic and religious diversity.

In the introduction to her important volume *La Relation à l'Autre* (The Relation to the Other), French sociologist Dominique Schnapper stresses "the difficulty of pursuing objective analysis when it comes to exploring subjects that affect the legitimacy of our social and political order."[1] Comparisons between national models of integration necessarily mobilize, at some level, the judgments of those who are doing the comparing—judgments that favor one concrete model or another, or a given set of principles or ideals. As I will try to show, certain images of the French and U.S. models that appear in political debate and even in scholarly analysis are misleading, and in politically significant ways.

I do not claim here to occupy a neutral stance in the comparison between the two models. It will be clear from my argumentation that I find certain key features of the French model more satisfying from the point of view of social integration and equity than what the U.S. model can provide, if indeed any single model prevails in the United States, which is doubtful. It is also my purpose, however, to relativize the differences between the models—and the value judgments these differences inspire—by placing the models in their historical context and by considering their dynamics and potentialities. Value judgments about models of citizenship are inevitable, but it is preferable that they not be formulated through frames of reference mechanically transposed from other models. It is preferable that they be grounded in informed assessments of the concrete political structures, forces, and dynamics within given nation-states and the sets of choices all these factors generate.

If monographic studies of single national models run the risk of becoming too self-referential and disconnected from the universe of possibilities, the same danger haunts comparative analysis that stays too attached to limited sets of given national examples. One path beyond such closure involves articulating, at the outset, the problems with which *all* national models of citizenship are necessarily confronted in a "globalized" economic, political, strategic, and cultural order. According to one argument frequently encountered in comparative analysis, national sovereignty is losing ground under the influence of multiple and irreversible transnational currents: financial flows, corporate strategies, transnational political constructions, media networks, and, last but not least, the affirmation within national societies of increasing ethnic and cultural diversity and the emergence of claims for the recognition of such diversity, sometimes through "multicultural citizenship" rights.[2] Full attention to all the processes related to globalization is beyond the scope of this essay, but my overall reaction to this type of formulation is that in spite of corrosive effects of globalization on national sovereignty, national models of integration have not spoken their last. Stronger, more institutionally ramified and verbally articulated models of national integration, such as the French one, cannot be dismissed as archaic and stubbornly opposed to the supposedly inevitable trends of globalization. The French model may still be capable, though admittedly under increasing economic and political strain, of providing, through the republican state, a rampart against social disintegration,[3] and for this reason it deserves more sympathetic understanding than it has received in recent years. The French model has frequently been painted by foreign commentators, and by a few domestic ones, as "assimilationist" or "ethnocentric,"[4] as if it were openly hostile to the expression of cultural diversity, and as if it could be taken for granted that a more multicultural model of citizenship is by definition more endowed with democratic virtues. My main concern here is to correct such misperceptions of the French model by showing, more accurately than has often been done, how it operates, though without attempting to deny that the model is in crisis (see the first section). Many of the negative judgments formulated about this model may simply evaporate once it is understood that it does not imply a frontal threat to diversity or the ethnocentric defense of a monolithic national culture. This is not to deny that the model has certain weaknesses, notably when it comes to fighting ethnoracial discrimination in the workplace. But even in this area, as I shall try to show, the French model is not without resources.

As for the U.S. mode of managing diversity (see the second section), it is never defended unconditionally, and sometimes rejected outright, by French commentators. The grounds on which such judgments are formulated are sometimes solidly documented but often less so. From the point of view of those who staunchly defend the French model, there is indeed much to criticize in the prevailing U.S. model. Affirmative action, battles over school curricula waged in the name of an often ill-defined "multiculturalism," and the excesses of "political correctness" are taken—not altogether correctly, I would argue—as signs of a society and polity that often place such a great emphasis on "identity" and "difference" that it becomes difficult to conceive of a common ground on which a project of social integration can be built. However, these typically American phenomena are sometimes lumped together abusively and taken as evidence that U.S. society is so obsessed with ethnic difference that no openings whatsoever are possible toward a more universalistic mode of politics—a notion I take to be not unfounded but somewhat exaggerated. In short, just as unduly harsh assessments of the French model err by lack of understanding of the recognition it indeed gives to cultural diversity, blanket condemnations of U.S. reality too often ignore the ways in which, in spite of all the ambient fragmentation, forms of "transethnic" and even "postethnic" politics can sometimes emerge.

THE FRENCH CASE

Defining the French Republican Model of Citizenship

As has often been noted, the French model of citizenship places strict limits on the ways and contexts in which the state may accord attention to the ethnicity or religion of individuals. The French model assumes that while citizens are free to cultivate, in the private sphere, any religious practices, languages, or ethnic heritages they please, the public sphere, and in particular the sphere of politics, should be kept free whenever possible of cleavages based on differences of origin. Unlike in the United States, citizens are not classified by ethnic origin or in official statistics or in the national census, and this rule (recently contested by some social scientists) reflects political and constitutional principles that are deeply rooted in an articulated republican conception of the nation. As one obvious example of the political consequences that flow from such a model, affirmative action as a method of struggle against ethnic or racial discrimination cannot be a policy option in France (I shall return to this problem later).

The vocation of the republic is to remain united, in the sense that democratic conflicts over social choices should be channeled into and treated by democratic institutions without interference from ethnic or religious particularisms. The state adheres, by law and by constitutional writ, to the idea of *laïcité*, which refers not just to the separation of church and state but more broadly to an official neutrality that is intended to guarantee the pluralism of religious beliefs and practices in the private sphere even while barring manifestations of such particularisms in the public sphere.

A strong and active republican state is an essential ingredient of this model because of the state's indispensable role in guaranteeing social cohesion and solidarity. Inequalities must not become so pronounced (or, by implication, so ethnically conditioned), that they take on a dimension of systematic oppression against given categories of citizens (or noncitizens). Solidarity is achieved not only through equality of civil and political rights but also through policies that guarantee decent levels of economic and social well-being.

In such a model, populations of different national, religious, or ethnic origins are discouraged from forming ethnic lobbies in the public sphere; they must not claim rights based on ethnic particularism or cultural difference; they must avoid turning religious or ethnic solidarities into permanent instruments of political mobilization. Mobilization along particularist lines is referred to, in the French vocabulary of citizenship, as *communautarisme*, and the term has a pointedly negative connotation. *Communautarisme* refers, at the individual level, to behavior which "privileges ethnic, religious, racial or tribal belonging over inter-human, collective solidarity."[5] At the political level it could be defined as the grouping together of people of common ethnic or national origins or common religious affiliations into organizations that make particularist claims on the state or on political parties. When allowed to go unchecked, *communautarisme* is seen as harboring strong potential for derailing the political life of the republic (i.e., provoking divisions among citizens along particularist lines and obscuring democratic debate over universalist goals and social visions for the future of the national society).

Choices about models of social and economic regulation are fair game for democratic debate and competition, but when such choices take on ethnic connotations, or when ethnicity itself becomes an obsessional issue in public debate, something is badly amiss in the republic. Those who have most ethnicized the French public sphere in recent years are the right-wing populist leaders of the National Front, who, while borrowing selectively from republican rhetoric, denature its meaning by promoting a conception of the French nation that is ethnic rather than civic. The success they have had up to now (and in spite of the recent split between the Le Pen and Mégret factions) is one key sign that the republican model is in crisis. However, there is much controversy as to the nature and the causes of this crisis—a problem to which I shall return later.

It is not by chance that in France rarely is any reference made to "ethnic minorities," because the very notion would suggest that such groups are constituted into "communities," with the vocation of playing a role as such in the public sphere. Only foreign commentators regularly refer to France's immigrant populations as "minorities," taking it for granted that the vocabulary used in the United States or Britain is appropriate to the French situation.[6]

Laïcité and Education

Understanding the French model requires some familiarity with the principle of *laïcité* and with the policies that have been adopted over the past two hundred years in its name.[7] Few other countries have carved out, through the political process, such a highly rationalized set of rules and institutions dedicated to defining the relations between organized religions and the state. Such efforts are not undertaken simply to prevent the domination of one religion over others but more generally to ensure that the public sphere remains a sphere of democratic discourse rather than becoming dominated by exclusivist or ethnicizing logics.

Most defenders of the republican model do not deny that some partisans of *laïcité* have wielded the idea in a rigid and doctrinaire way. In the late nineteenth and early twentieth centuries, pro-*laïcité* sentiment frequently took the form of radical anticlericalism, and today, the heirs to this approach have taken some unconditional stands on central matters of interest—most famously, in recent years, on the wearing of the Islamic headscarf by young women in public schools (a problem to be discussed later). However, *laïcité* has usually been more open-ended, and its defense has been based on negotiation rather than on authoritarian injunctions.

Champions of *laïcité* have never formed a united bloc. They have recently disagreed among themselves as to whether safeguarding the neutrality of the public

sphere necessarily means excluding *all* manners of particularism from its midst
or whether such neutrality should, rather, be forged in a public dialogue involving the representatives of ethnic associations, in the shared aim of defining a common ground. Once it is admitted that some or most existing forms of ethnic or religious particularism can be prodded toward a more universalistic vision through
dialogue, the next logical step is to acknowledge that diversity is not *in itself* a
threat to democratic citizenship but must be "worked with" in the effort to forge
a more democratic public sphere.

Contrary to what is often imagined, there is no necessary contradiction between the republican and *laïque* model and the promotion of "intercultural" education in the public school system.[8] The well-known report *L'Intégration à la
française* issued by the *Haut Conseil à l'Intégration* in the early 1990s,[9] one of
the central reference documents for recent debates about the model, devotes an
important subchapter to the subject of "The Encounter of the Cultures." The passage begins as follows: "If school has a crucial role to play in the process of integrating immigrants . . . it is also the place where a rich dialogue can be engaged
among children and parents about the diversity of cultural contributions."[10] The
authors of the report admit that for a long time, the "Jacobin and uniformizing
French tradition" called for "erasing differences rather than exalting them," and
they recognize that this tradition led to certain classic absurdities such as history
lessons in which children of different origins were all taught that "Our ancestors
were Gauls." They go on to applaud the Ministry of National Education for "taking into account the growing diversity of French society in its instructions and
teaching programs."[11]

The term *interculturalité*, which designates the sharing of knowledge and the
development of mutual trust among people of different cultural origins, is used in
France in clear distinction to *multiculturalism*. Indeed, the French model does not
extend to "multicultural citizenship," defined as a system of rights open to people of designated ethnic origins or religious beliefs, whether such rights be related
to socioeconomic opportunity or to the quest for cultural recognition. Diversity
can be accepted and even valued at many levels in the French model, but ethnic
or religious particularisms cannot become a parameter in determining who governs, who represents voters, how resources are allocated, or how public services
(in particular the school system) are run. Of course, over more than a century of
practice in defending the neutrality of the state with respect to the diverse religions, French governing officials have developed a complex set of rules that
place limits on particularist claims without claiming to ban their expression altogether in authoritarian fashion. For example, most school cafeterias make an effort to cater to the needs of pupils who respect the Jewish and Islamic prohibition
on pork. Given that the school calendar recognizes many Christian holidays, occasional absences for the major holidays of other religions are acceptable, but the
line is drawn when the school system itself is disrupted—for example, when or-
thodox Jewish parents request permission to keep their children out of school

every Saturday, or when Muslim families seek to withdraw their daughters from physical or sexual education classes.[12]

The Islamic Headscarf Affair

The question of the Islamic headscarf in school became a burning public issue in September 1989, when three young girls enrolled in the Collège Gabriel-Havez in the town of Creil, north of Paris, were suspended from school by their principal on the grounds that their use of religious symbols was a form of proselytism and thus incompatible with the rules of *laïcité*. This affair became a symbol, nationally and internationally, of France's tribulations in dealing with immigrants, but what exactly the affair symbolized was not always so clear, since it lent itself to a confusing array of interpretations. For some outside observers, what it revealed was simply official French intolerance of diversity, in particular regarding Islam and North African immigrants.[13] This is an abusive interpretation, as I shall attempt to show.

The real and unavoidable ambiguity in the 1989 headscarf affair had to do with the diversity of opinions and sensibilities on *both* sides of the issue (i.e., among those who opposed the wearing of the headscarf as well as among those who believed it should be tolerated). Opponents included people of a broad range of opinion, from highly dogmatic exponents of *laïcité* (including no small number of teachers), people suspicious of Islam itself, and more moderate defenders of *laïcité* who were indeed torn between the principle of strict religious neutrality in the school system and the principle of tolerance of diverse cultural practices. The principal of the school, a man of French Caribbean origin, later revealed himself to be straddling the first two categories. As for those who defended the right to wear the headscarf, their side, too, sheltered a wide spectrum of sensibilities, from a tiny minority of fundamentalist Muslims and a larger number of moderate Muslims, to defenders of a more flexible version of *laïcité*, which continued to oppose the use of religious symbols in school but preferred that any decision to prohibit the headscarf be taken only after ample dialogue with the young women and families concerned. On both sides of the issue were defenders of women's rights: one the one hand, those who saw the headscarf as a symbol of the subordination of women in Muslim tradition and, on the other, those who believed that in spite of this subordination, the opinions of the young girls should be taken into account through dialogue.

Although it is undeniable that sectors of the French population are suspicious of Islam in general and that this suspicion is deeply rooted in French history, it would be a gross exaggeration to take the headscarf affair as a sign that France as a whole, and its official institutions in particular, have turned Islam into a scapegoat. This position is untenable for two main reasons. First, the official solution that was adopted for the 1989 headscarf affair by order of the Conseil d'État, and which has been applied to similar affairs since then, has involved

dialogue and mediation rather than authoritarian measures of expulsion—
except between 1994 and 1997, when the orders issued by then Minister of Education François Bayrou, a conservative, resulted in harsher treatment, including numerous suspensions of pupils.[14] When the left returned to power in 1997,
there was a return to a policy of negotiation, using the services of an official
mediator, Madame Hanifa Cherifi.

Second, the development of Islam itself is not an issue for the French state. It
is true, once again, that a few opponents of the headscarf, hiding behind slogans
of radical *laïcité*, are more suspicious of Islam itself than they are concerned
about specific violations of the norms of *laïcité*. It is also undeniably true that in
certain cities and towns in France, attempts by local Muslim associations to build
mosques have been treated with open hostility or at least great suspicion. In several of these cities, mosques have nonetheless been opened. This is true because
the French state, including governments of both the left and right over the past
fifteen years, have made a strong effort to favor the integration of Islam into
French society. Official policy involves helping Muslims to organize their religious institutions in a way that entirely respects the pluralism implicit in the idea
of *laïcité*. Measures taken have included providing funds to facilitate the ritual
slaughter of sheep, under acceptable conditions of sanitation, for the feast of Aïd
el Kébir.

One respect in which this effort to promote the integration of Islam has been
disappointing has been the failure, up to now, to create a permanent dialogue between the state and recognized representatives of Islam, as exists for other religions. However, the main reason for this failure has been the Muslims' own lack
of success in designating leaders recognized by all its associations as representative.[15] Islamic associations of all sorts have flourished in France, in particular
since the 1981 law that authorized foreigners to create associations according to
the same legal rules as applies to nationals, but the very diversity (including ethnic diversity) among these associations has made it extremely difficult to determine who should represent the religion as a whole.

Since they are located at a vital intersection between the private sphere and the
public sphere, associations occupy an important place in what many social scientists and philosophers refer to as civil society. It happens that in France, all associations must be registered with the police, in order that the state may be informed, if necessary, of the activities of given associations, for any reason,
ranging from the most banal legal dispute among the association's members to
the political activities of the more militant associations. Since a very few associations, including some Islamic ones, may harbor forms of political-religious fanaticism that threaten democracy with violent disruption, it is understandable that
the state should wish to keep tabs on these. Active surveillance does not extend
to ordinary associations for the promotion of religious culture. Clearly, however,
the state seeks to favor those tendencies—which make up a clear majority of existing Muslim associations—that accept the rules of *laïcité* and disseminate Islam

as an individualized religious faith rather than as an instrument of collective political mobilization for authoritarian causes.

Can the French Model Deal with Ethnic Discrimination?

The struggle against ethnic discrimination in the workplace may be the single greatest weak spot of the French republican model as it has functioned up to now. It is true that the model's relegation of ethnic and religious identities to the private sphere severely restricts the classification of citizens by origin and therefore renders impossible any form of ethnically based affirmative action. Although this restriction closes one major route to the struggle against discrimination, it also aims at limiting ethnic fragmentation, which remains anathema to the model in its ideal form and serves, practically speaking, to channel politics into choices about problems of more universal import.

Even if there were significant political support in France for affirmative action, which there is not, it would be strictly impossible to conceive of such a policy, simply because the population is not officially classified by ethnic origin. An affirmative action program cannot work without numbers, and such numbers are unavailable in France. It is almost impossible to generate them officially without violating a key founding constitutional principle of the modern French nation: the democratic, republican, and *laïque* character of the national bond. This question of ethnic statistics has given rise, in the past few years, to a great controversy that first involved a small group of social scientists but has now come directly into the political arena, in the context of a debate over what kinds of remedies can indeed be found to discrimination if affirmative action is not an option. Researchers at the national institute of demography, INED, have become bitterly divided over the issue, which could be framed as follows: is it contrary to the spirit of the republic to gather of statistics about the ethnicity of individuals in connection with other parameters such as professional status and level of education, on the grounds that these could contribute to the formation of stereotypes, or can such statistics indeed be useful, in spite of such potentially invidious uses, in forming an idea of how discrimination actually operates?[16] The fact is that statistics to measure discrimination are coming more and more into use.

It would be thus be unfair and incorrect to say that the French republican model of integration is incapable of generating analysis and treatment of the problem of discrimination. Since 1997, several studies have appeared about the forms and extent of discrimination in France, including official reports which recognize the full gravity of the problem and open new paths of reflection about possible remedies.[17] The socialist government under Prime Minister Lionel Jospin (1997–) has expressed the will to tackle the problem, though it is too early to say what mature form new remedies will take or how effective they can be. The main orientation for the moment is to apply existing laws with greater vigor, possibly under the authority of an oversight council and/or under the supervision of mixed commissions of public and "civil society" actors.[18]

The logic of the republican model makes it necessary, of course, to frame remedies to discrimination in terms of universal rights of all citizens, not as a system of differential rights for different categories of citizens. Within these limits, how effectively can antidiscriminatory laws be enforced? From a juridical point of view, the French problem is in its essence quite similar to what it has been in the United States when affirmative action has come under attack: to prosecute for discrimination and to obtain a settlement, victims of discrimination must be able to show *intent* to discriminate. This is just as difficult in France as elsewhere, since employers have many ways of disguising their discriminatory intent. Nonetheless, dissuading employers from practicing discrimination does not necessarily involve systematic ethnic classification; institutionalized vigilance over employers' practices can be made more effective without resorting to affirmative action.

It should be added that the French public policy has developed certain "functional equivalents" of affirmative action in the areas of education, urban development, vocational guidance, and others; they do not target given ethnic groups but strive rather to combat inequalities linked to residence in given geographic zones. Zones designated for special compensatory treatment may indeed be more densely populated by immigrants or their descendants, but ethnicity is clearly subordinated, in the language and (usually) in the spirit of policymakers, to more universal concerns linked to socioeconomic equity.[19]

Crisis of the French Republican Model or Crisis of the Social Fabric as a Whole?

Is the republican model of integration in crisis, as many claim? It cannot be denied that this is so. But what is the nature of this crisis? The interpretation of the model's crisis is itself a terrain of legitimate debate, and the views expressed have sometimes been sharply contradictory. Some would claim that the model itself has outlived its usefulness and proven too rigid, on the grounds that it has failed to grant enough spaces of democratic expression for ethnic particularism, in an era when nation-states can no longer claim to exercise tight control over the formation of identities and loyalties. However, one never hears calls for a radical multiculturalist pluralism in France. Those who have contested the republican model's "rigidities" have done so in the name of republican values, expressing, like Michel Wieviorka[20] or Joel Roman,[21] the hope that ethnic subjectivities freely expressed in the public sphere can be contained within limits well short of a confrontational ethnic politics or *communautarisme*.

The other major interpretation of the crisis is based on the idea that the crisis is not due to the republican model's own inherent rigidity but rather to a much broader crisis of social integration that needs to be addressed on its own terms, with an emphasis on developing social policies that contribute to greater equality among all categories of the population, and on the development of active or participatory citizenship toward this end.[22]

Both sides would agree on an essential point: The so-called "immigrant problem" in French politics, as it emerged starting in the early 1980s, was largely an ideological construction, symptomatic of the broader crisis affecting France's mechanisms of social integration. If immigrants were turned into scapegoats by a racist populist movement (including but not limited to the National Front), this scapegoat effect needs to be explained in turn with reference to the forms of social distress and political disaffiliation that have affected broad categories of citizens and made them receptive to the sirens of the nationalist far right. In other words, there is no understanding the development of racism outside the context of the unemployment crisis, the problem of unequal access to education, and social exclusion in all its guises.

Nor is the social crisis in France a simple matter of socioeconomic factors, as most would agree, but also a profound crisis of political representation. Political parties in general have greater trouble than ever mobilizing broad sectors of the population around defined political programs; there is a sharp drop in levels of public confidence regarding the capacity of political parties and governing coalitions, once in power, to produce tangible change.

The principal difference between the two interpretations turns on the practical question of how to combat racism and xenophobia. Those who advocate limited doses of multiculturalism believe that this would be one way, if not necessarily the main way, of containing or channeling the resentment of young people, immigrants, or children of immigrants, who are victims of racism and exclusion. Opponents of this approach believe that significant concessions to the differential logic of multiculturalism would not only undermine the values of the republic but also play into the hands of the racist right, which is constantly seeking ways to demonstrate that immigrants constitute a special interest group and that the "real" victims of discrimination are the "French" themselves (read: white and of Christian origin).

In its early days, in the 1980s, the association "SOS-Racisme" campaigned among French youth using the slogan "the right to difference" (*le droit à la différence*) but soon abandoned this rhetoric and adopted a language of republican integration and citizenship rights. The reason for this shift was that the association came under sharp criticism from intellectuals and political activists who saw great risks in the differentialist approach. The danger, as expressed by Pierre-André Taguieff, among others, was that the antiracist differentialism of movement activists would feed into the differentialist "neoracism" professed by the National Front.[23] What is differentialist racism? It is a kind of discourse, common to many European right-wing movements, that no longer refers (explicitly, at least) to a supposed superiority of whites or Christians over other "races" but instead celebrates difference and uses it as an argument for separation based on the incompatibility of different cultures. Jean-Marie Le Pen has frequently declared his love of Maghrebi culture, provided that it stays at home in the Maghreb and does not "contaminate" the French nation. Taguieff's argument, shared by all those who defend the republican model, is that the terrain of the nation should not be left to the racist right but rather defended as the common ground on which citizens of all origins can contribute to the building of a better society.

Naturally, this idea is condemned to failure if it remains at the level of principles. What is needed is not just the ideal of a *res publica* for all citizens regardless of ethnic origins but abundant democratic activity, from "above" and from "below," aiming at solving the social problems that are sources of frustration and create a favorable atmosphere for the development of racism and violence: severe inequality in education, high unemployment, poorly maintained public housing, employment discrimination, mistrust between youths and the police, and so forth.

Let us conclude this brief survey of the French model with two observations. First, the restrictions placed on the cultural, linguistic, and religious practices of foreigners are less severe in the actual practice of this model than many observers believe. The model is by no means contradictory, as we have seen, with tolerance of diverse cultural practices in the private sphere and "intercultural" policies and discourses in the public sphere. Second, the defense of the model is conceived, by those who most ardently aspire to keep it alive, not just as a defense of the "nation" in the abstract but as a defense of the social bond itself. The premise is that the republican state is the best rampart against a transnational, neoliberal capitalism that threatens, if unchecked, to dissolve existing mechanisms of social integration. The point is certainly not to close off France to the influences of foreign cultures, which is neither possible (as the racist right imagines) nor desirable, but rather to channel the energies of all citizens into forms of democratic activity that can resist the socially corrosive effects of neoliberal capitalism. This channeling of energies requires, as Sami Naïr puts it, turning differences of origin into something banal, to be subsumed under a common sense of belonging,[24] and this is perhaps the best short summary of what the republican model stands for.

THE CENTRALITY OF ETHNIC CONSCIOUSNESS IN THE UNITED STATES

Is there a U.S. model of integration of diversity? In an important sense, there is none, because many of the parameters of such a model vary from state to state and from institution to institution. The relative coherence of the French model cannot be assumed in the U.S. case because the U.S. political system, with its federal structure and its weaker state from the standpoint of social integration, makes it possible for a patchwork of different discourses and practices to coexist and, frequently, to confront each other.

The "U.S. model," as evoked in French political discourse or social science analysis, usually refers to one particularly salient trait of U.S. reality: the official recognition of ethnic difference and the fragmentation of society into ethnically defined groups that tendentially crystallize into communities or even political blocs, thereby polarizing the political sphere along particularist lines. In this respect, from the French republican point of view, the U.S. model appears in many ways to be the very example, among the rich Western countries, of what to avoid.

Is the United States a "multicultural" country? When observed from afar, the controversies related to affirmative action, school curricula, and "political correctness" all tend to blend together, especially in the minds of stricter exponents of the French republican model, into the hazy image of a country where the valorization of ethnic difference has run amok, creating fragmentation everywhere in the name of what Denis Lacorne calls "multicultural passions."[25] No French commentator has proposed the U.S. model as an unequivocally positive example for France. At most, those authors who call for a slightly greater "dose" of multiculturalism in France try to attenuate the negative image of U.S. reality by suggesting that the United States should not be used as a "scarecrow."[26]

However the image of the U.S. is mobilized in French debates over the management of diversity, there is scant knowledge of how ethnic politics in the United States actually operates. There is a tendency to generalize on the basis of the knowledge of a few cases—the Nation of Islam under Louis Farrakhan, Afrocentric curricula, the Ebonics controversy, among others—and to see in these cases symbols of *communautarisme*. In a recent article, Michel Wieviorka makes a useful distinction between "integrated" systems of multicultural rights (such as those of Canada, Australia, and Sweden) and "fragmented" ones, a category to which the United States belongs, and this certainly represents progress over vaguer images of "multicultural passions."[27]

The logic of the French republican model would lead one to suspect that ethnically based political mobilizations lead necessarily and directly to *communautarisme* and its attendant woes. It is undeniably true that ethnic politics in the U.S. has a fragmenting affect, but it is equally true that there have been in recent U.S. experience a few attempts to move beyond ethnic politics and build democratic coalitions based on social and economic programs of universal import. There is scant knowledge in French research of how the logic of political coalitions can operate in such a way as to relativize or subsume ethnic discourses and claims under the umbrella of broader political groupings. The necessities of coalition building—for example, efforts by African Americans or Hispanics to establish a place within the Democratic Party—often places limits on the particularist appeals of leaders claiming to represent a given ethnic group. Such logic operates with some effectiveness in certain cities and states, as a few researchers have revealed,[28] but little is known about the broad range of experiences within the patchwork universe of the United States.

THE FRENCH REPUBLICAN
MODEL MEETS AFFIRMATIVE ACTION

As one can easily imagine, French commentators often take a very dim view of U.S.-style affirmative action, for reasons related to the principles of the republican model. The value judgments they formulate about affirmative action are frequently based on an inadequate knowledge of how it actually works. For example, affirmative action is sometimes equated with "quotas" by authors who forget that that a key Supreme Court decision (*Regents of the University of California v. Bakke,* 1978) made rigid systems of quotas strictly unconstitutional.[29] It is true that an emerging body of work has begun to fill in major gaps in understanding about the workings of affirmative action.[30]

The key objection to affirmative action voiced by numerous French commentators is that it is based on a system of ethnic and racial classification that tends to perpetuate itself and thus contribute powerfully to an ongoing logic of differentiation. Dominique Schnapper writes that "what we may call the ethnic welfare state . . . inevitably contributes to creating and maintaining ethnic consciousness, mobilizing ethnic groups as political forces and thus organizing the social structure according to the existence of these groups." She does recognize extenuating circumstances: "Unfortunately, American history has also demonstrated that blacks have not obtained equality of treatment or opportunities by struggling, from Du Bois to Martin Luther King, in the name of universalistic principles of American democracy which are at the foundations of a policy of equal opportunity."[31]

Denis Lacorne, a knowledgeable historian of identity politics in the United States, professes his opposition, on republican grounds, to all forms of official racial or ethnic classification: "The state must be color-blind, as the Supreme Court justices never stop repeating."[32] Some of his objections to affirmative action are based on the idea that the U.S. state does not do its job of assuring a minimum of social integration: "Affirmative action would not exist if the high schools of big cities fulfilled correctly their role of education and formation of citizens."[33] In this respect, affirmative action is in Lacorne's view a conservative remedy against discrimination, in that it favors middle-class blacks over those who are more disadvantaged in the competition for jobs. He would clearly prefer that affirmative action not exist and that a republican state instead fulfill its function of social integration, but he allows nonetheless that affirmative action might have some justification in the case of African Americans, as long as the policy is clearly defined as being limited in time.[34]

In spite of this proviso, which he grants in the name of a "moderate" or "republicanized" multiculturalism, Lacorne's basic reasoning about affirmative action collides with arguments in U.S. philosophical circles to the effect that to reach the end of a "color-blind" society, it is necessary to adopt "color-conscious" remedies in the fight against discrimination.[35] He understands that affirmative action, in spite of the intractable political dilemmas it has engendered because of its differentialist logic, is one of the few existing mechanisms for fighting inequalities due to racial discrimination. Yet he does not recognize that affirmative action is defended against attack by some in the United States who (like him) do not see it by any means as an ideal system for combating inequalities and would admit that socioeconomic or need-based criteria should be combined with racial criteria in deciding who should benefit and to what extent.[36] Scant attention is paid by Lacorne, as by most French commentators, to the alternatives that would await African Americans if affirmative action were simply abolished or at least severely restricted in its scope, which is, of course, increasingly the case. The political choice as to whether or not to defend affirmative action is, of course, conditioned by this horizon of possibility, not just by philosophical arguments about the principle of color-blindness.

THE U.S. SITUATION IN HISTORICAL PERSPECTIVE

The example of the United States has become such a frequent reference in French debates over ethnic diversity and citizenship that some authors have reached beyond the immediacy of current polemics in an effort to place the U.S. model in its historical context. After all, it is impossible to explain the omnipresence of race and ethnicity in the United States without returning to the origins of this society in English colonial times. Those French authors who take a long historical view are well aware that much can be explained by the logics of radical exclusion that were already at work against Native Americans and African slaves in early colonial times and, somewhat later, against Mexicans, who became engulfed in a quasi-colonial relationship with the conquerors of the western frontier.[37]

In *La Crise de l'identité américaine* (1997), Denis Lacorne has captured in a pithy formula a great contradiction which defines U.S. history: the United States, he says, is an "ethno-civic" nation, "civic by inclusion and ethnic by exclusion."[38] In other words, there is a sharp and constant clash between the principles of democratic tolerance written into the U.S. Constitution at the republic's foundation, and the concrete and often radical forms of ethnoracial exclusion that have constantly betrayed these principles. The principles have chalked up some stunning democratic triumphs, but the logics of exclusion have also continued apace, in constantly evolving forms.

Lacorne's reading of U.S. history is one long and well-informed illustration of this contradiction. His accounts of the different waves of nativist sentiment and his analysis of the image of the melting pot are masterful.[39] However, in one important respect, his reading of history breaks down. The closer his analysis draws to the current era, the more he becomes embroiled in contemporary controversies, and the more his reading of history becomes clouded by value judgments whose pertinence to the U.S. situation is debatable. In a nutshell, the problem is as follows: for Lacorne, the civil rights movement, with its central demand of full citizenship rights, was "republican" and universalistic in all its implications. Demands for affirmative action, multicultural curricula, and the like appear in his reading as a betrayal of this republican moment in U.S. politics, and he attributes this betrayal to the power of "multicultural passions"—a factor of irrationality, as opposed to republican rationality.[40] It could easily be pointed out, in contradiction to this reading, that many ingrown, sectarian, and separatist ethnic movements can be found in U.S. history well before the civil rights movement. The Nation of Islam, to take one example, was founded in the 1930s, and, in spite of its frequent changes in leadership and orientation, it has been a constant presence in many cities since then, regardless of the civil rights movement. The existence of such a sect, or of the Marcus Garvey movement, or of nineteenth-century African colonization movements, are not so much the fruit of "multicultural passions" as reactions to racism in times when the prospects of socioeconomic and political integration seemed distant. Today's Afrocentrism is in many ways not so new; it manifests a reflex of withdrawal into particularism that has long existed, and for reasons having much to do with the racism and exclusion that continue in spite of the emergence of a solid black middle class. Lacorne is well aware of these phenomena and does not fail to mention them in his historical account. The problem is not an inadequate knowledge of history but rather a tendency to mechanically transpose the republican model onto U.S. reality.

FROM MODELS OF CITIZENSHIP TO MODELS OF SOCIETY

To Lacorne and like-minded observers, the United States today looks like a morass of particularisms, a land forsaken by the grace of republican virtues. In many ways they are right, yet some countertendencies deserve attention. David Hollinger has attempted to show, in *Post-Ethnic America: Beyond Multiculturalism*,[41] that forces are at work in U.S. society that could conceivably lead it, one day, "beyond ethnicity," via what he calls "the diversification of diversity." Ethnic identities, to which multiculturalists are so attached, need no longer be conceived as being automatically attributable to given individuals and groups as a function of their origins; identities, he argues, are kaleidoscopic constructions that can be, and are increasingly, a question of personal affinity. Although clearly the stigma attached to blackness in the United States escapes this postethnic logic, it, too, can become at least partially dissolved. The movement of citizens who wish to create a "mixed race" category in the national census is one modest but significant example.

Lacorne expresses some sympathy with the spirit of Hollinger's postethnic perspective,[42] yet he is openly skeptical about it, because he considers to be a flight into the imaginary. He writes:

By seeking to radically dissociate the civic and ethnic dimensions of the American identity, the theoreticians of a post-ethnic America commit an error of historical understanding. They forget that the American citizen does not aspire, in general, unless he is forced, to become a "100% American." He remains an "ethnic," that is, he is often conscious of his national, religious or cultural origins.[43]

Lacorne seems to miss a major point made by Hollinger—that overcoming ethnic and racial barriers is not just a question of individual choice but also a question of social dynamics and movements. In a way that sometimes recalls the republican model, *mutatis mutandis*, Hollinger calls for a rehabilitation, in the United States, of the *civic nation*—that is, a common ground on which people of all origins, having taken distance from their ethnic and religious "identities," can work together in pursuit of common social goals.[44] This cannot just happen by wishing it; it requires a redefinition of social goals in a social-democratic direction, and concrete action to achieve them, in order that those groups that have been excluded may indeed have some reason to feel they are included in the "we" of the nation. In a country where a Democratic president has adopted large portions of the Republican neoliberal program, there is indeed room for skepticism, yet it is at least worthwhile to point out the few actions and movements that point in a different direction. Lacorne understands that Hollinger is calling for a nation-state that directs much more of its energies to the struggle against poverty and socioeconomic inequalities, but he remains unconvinced by the vision, on the grounds that it does not clearly define the "articulation between the civic foundations of the American nation and the persistence of ethnocultural preoccupations, between the universal and the particular, between the *Unum* and the *Pluribus*."[45] Such an articulation would, in Lacorne's view, have to address the problems raised by philosophers such as Michael Sandel and Michael Walzer—representing two different varieties of "communitarian" thinking—such as how to incite individuals to become more involved in public affairs, how to constitute a fabric of local, regional, and national forms of engagement, how to build a civil society.

At this level of generality, it must be admitted that Lacorne raises here a legitimate and eminently open question about the fate of citizenship itself, in a country suffering from a "crisis of republicanism." It could be remarked, however, that if Lacorne were really interested in looking for concrete examples of inter- or transethnic alliances forged through democratic social movements that push the state toward greater social engagement, he could find them.[46] They are not abundant, and they certainly do not represent a dominant trend in U.S. society, but they exist and can be seen, if one wishes, as a potentiality to be built upon. To look for a French-style republican state in the United States is clearly a futile exercise, but struggles that may lead in a slightly more "republican" direction should not be neglected.

The question of the United States' "model" of citizenship—or lack of one—ultimately leads, as the foregoing debate suggests, to the broader question of the U.S. overall social model, which might be defined briefly as the mode by which the state (at all levels, federal, state, and local) contributes or not to the overall cohesion of society, not just in ethnic terms but in socioeconomic terms as well. In this respect, French social science research has made important strides, thanks to the work of sociologists such as Loïc Wacquant[47] and, in a slightly different vein, Sophie Body-Gendrot.[48] How do the racial segregation of cities (the ghetto effect), the racial stereotyping of "welfare mothers" or the severe overrepresentation of African Americans in U.S. prisons reflect a more general model of social exclusion? By raising questions at this level, these authors have contributed more to the understanding of the U.S. model of citizenship than any number of studies exclusively about diversity issues. Wacquant supports with a wealth of empirical data his central contention that the French social model, in spite of its growing difficulties, is still far from the "war of all against all" that characterizes social life in the United States.

CONCLUSION

In attempting to combat certain misconceptions regarding both the French and U.S. models of integration, my more general purpose here has been to advocate a more historicized and contextualized understanding of each national model. Such a perspective does not preclude value judgments about these models, but it does encourage more circumspect judgments, grounded in the politically possible.

Analyzing the French republican model in the light of preconceptions about its supposed ethnocentric character leads not only to a misreading of how the model actually works in practice, but to a certain blindness regarding one of its leading contemporary rationales. That rationale is to resist, insofar as possible, the social disintegration provoked by neoliberal capitalism—a disintegration that could arguably be exacerbated by differentialist or multiculturalist approaches to the management of ethnic and religious diversity, particularly when confronted with a strong right-wing, racist movement that has not hesitated, as we have seen, to make its own use of differentialist discourse.

By the same token, transposing mechanically onto the reading of U.S. reality the norms of the French republican model can result in serious misunderstandings of how the fragmented U.S. "model" of integration actually works. The undeniable predominance of differentialist logics in many sectors does not mean that there is no potential whatsoever for a more universalistic agenda promoted by actors capable of transcending their particularisms.

NOTES

1. Dominique Schnapper, *La Relation à l'Autre: Au cœur de la pensée sociologique* (Paris: Gallimard, 1998), 19.

2. Such concerns are expressed in a wide range of recent works, including Riva Kastoryano, ed., *Quelle identité pour l'Europe?* *Le Multiculturalisme à l'épreuve* (Paris: Presses de Sciences Po, 1998); Michel Wieviorka, ed., *Une Société fragmentée? Le Multiculturalisme en débat* (Paris: La Découverte, 1996); several other works by Michel Wieviorka, including *La Démocratie à l'épreuve: Nationalisme, populisme, ethnicité* (Paris: La Découverte, 1993); and T. Modood and P. Werbner, eds., *The Politics of Multiculturalism in the New Europe: Racism, Identity and Community* (London/New York: Zed, 1997).

3. For an important and nuanced defense of the French model, see Sami Naïr, *Le Regard des vainqueurs: Les Enjeux français de l'immigration* (Paris: Grasset, 1992). In a slightly different vein, see the numerous works of Pierre-André Taguieff, including the recent *Face au Front national: Arguments pour une contre-offensive* (Paris: La Découverte, 1998), written with Michèle Tribalat, in which the authors defend the framework of the French nation-state as a potentially effective one both for fighting anti-immigrant racism and for promoting social integration.

4. See, for example, Umberto Melotti in "International Migration in Europe: Social Projects and Political Cultures," in *The Politics of Multiculturalism in the New Europe: Racism, Identity and Community,* ed. T. Modood and P. Werbner (London: Zed, 1997); Max Silverman, "The Revenge of Civil Society: State, Nation and Society in France" in *Citizenship, Nationality and Migration in Europe,* ed. David Cesarani and Mary Fulbrook (London: Routledge, 1996); several of the contributions to Alec G. Hargreaves and Mark McKinney, eds., *Post-Colonial Cultures in France* (London: Routledge, 1997). In Alec G. Hargreaves's own book, *Immigration, "Race" and Ethnicity in Contemporary France* (London: Routledge, 1994), judgments of this kind are occasionally formulated but are tempered by meticulous attention to how the French model actually works. Among French writers who draw inspiration from foreign criticisms of the French model, we may cite Joël Roman, "Un Multiculturalisme à la française?" *Esprit* (June 1995): 145-60, and the works by Michel Wieviorka cited in n. 2.

5. Naïr, *Le Regard des vainqueurs,* 210.

6. Several contributors to *Post-Colonial Cultures in France,* ed. Hargreaves and McKinney, refer to France's immigrants and their descendants as "minorities," but the term, I would argue, is employed out of context.

7. French analysts have produced large volumes of work about *laïcité,* its history, its actors, its evolving norms, and its continuing challenges. See, for example, Jacqueline Costa-Lascoux, *Les Trois âges de la laïcité* (Paris: Hachette, 1996); Guy Coq, *Laïcité et République, le lien nécessaire* (Paris: Editions du Félin, 1995); Guy Bedouelle and Jean-Paul Costa, *Les Laïcités à la française* (Paris: Presses Universitaires de France, 1998); the November 1995 issue of the journal *Pouvoirs* (no. 75); *Hommes et migrations,* special issue "Laïcité et diversité," nos. 1129-1130 (February–March 1990); *Hommes et migrations* 1218, "Laïcité, mode d'emploi" (March–April 1999); and many more.

8. Even a commentator such as Umberto Melotti, who takes a generally dim view of the French model on the grounds that it is "ethnocentric" and "assimilationist," admits that there is an "important debate regarding the possibility of introducing a new 'intercultural' approach to social life, and particularly in education." "International Migration in Europe," 78.

9. Published in book form by 10/18, 1993.

10. *L'Intégration à la française,* 118.

11. *L'Intégration à la française,* 117.

12. On this subject, see J. Costa-Lascoux, *Les Trois âges*, chap. 2, "Les Temps et les lieux du religieux."

13. Umberto Melotti buys into this interpretation; see "International Migration in Europe," 78, when he calls the treatment of Muslim girls in state schools "grotesque."

14. This period of relative official intolerance is related in a balanced way by Hargreaves in *Immigration, "Race" and Ethnicity*, 127–31.

15. This fact is generally acknowledged by all commentators. See, for example, Jocelyne Césari, "De l'islam en France à l'islam de France" in *Immigration et intégration: L'État des savoirs*, ed. Philippe Dewitte (Paris: La Découverte, 1999), 226, and A. Moustapha Diop, "Negotiating Religious Difference: The Opinions and Attitudes of Islamic Associations in France," in *The Politics of Multiculturalism*, ed. T. Modood and P. Werbner, 122–23.

16. The following press articles describe the main lines of this controversy: Nathaniel Herzberg, "Des chercheurs traquent les 'discriminations ethniques' dans le monde du travail,", *Le Monde*, 12 March 1996; Philippe Bernard and Nicolas Weill, "Une Virulente polémique sur les données 'ethniques' divise les démographes," *Le Monde*, 6 November 1998. Michèle Tribalat is one of the demographers directly involved in the controversy, because of her use of data about groups of immigrants by national origin in several key works of research, including *Faire France: Une Enquête sur les immigrés et leurs enfants* (Paris: La Découverte, 1995). She argues straightforwardly that such data contribute to the understanding of social reality and cannot be considered harmful in itself (see her editorial essay "La Connaissance des faits sociaux est-elle dangereuse?" *Le Monde*, 11 November 1998. Patrick Simon, a member of her research team, makes a significant contribution to the debate in "Sciences sociales et racisme, où sont les docteurs Folamour ?," *Mouvements* 3 (March–April 1999). Their main adversary is Hervé le Bras, another accomplished demographer who is adamantly opposed to ethnic data of any kind, in the name of the republican model, and on the grounds that such data can be exploited by groups such as the National Front and thereby contribute to the development of racism. His main contribution to the debate is a book entitled *Le Démon des origines* (Paris: Editions de l'Aube, 1998).

17. See Philippe Bataille, *Le Racisme au travail* (Paris: La Découverte, 1997); Haut Conseil à l'Intégration, report to the prime minister entitled *Lutte contre les discriminations: Faire respecter le principe d'égalité* (Paris: La Documentation Française, 1998). See also the report submitted by Conseiller d'État Jean-Michel Belorgey to the minister of employment and solidarity, 6 April 1999, calling for the creation of an "independent authority" comparable to the British Commission for Racial Equality (CRE).

18. For a description of nascent policy initiatives to combat discrimination, see *Hommes et migrations* 1219 (May–June 1999), an issue entitled "Connaître et combattre les discriminations."

19. An abundant literature exists in France on public policies based on such designation of geographic zones for special rehabilitative efforts. For the description of an interesting experiment in promoting employment for youth of North African origin, see Véronique de Rudder, Christian Poiret, François Vourc'h, "A Marseille, la 'préférence locale' contre les discriminations à l'embauche," *Hommes et migrations* 1211 (January–February 1998): 28–48. Véronique de Rudder and Christian Poiret openly challenge the republican model to translate equality of rights into equality of opportunities in "Affirmative Action et 'discrimination justifiée': Vers un universalisme en acte," in *Immigration et intégration*, ed. Dewitte.

20. Michel Wieviorka, *La Démocratie à l'épreuve*; Michel Wieviorka, ed., *Une Société fragmentée?* and several other works by this author in a similar vein.

21. Joël Roman, "Un Multiculturalisme à la française?" *Esprit* (June 1995): 145–60; "Pour un multiculturalisme tempéré," *Hommes et migrations* 1197 (April 1996): 18–22.

22. Sami Naïr, *Le Regard des vainqueurs*, and Pierre-André Taguieff, *Face au Front National*, develop this type of interpretation with greater clarity than most.

23. See Pierre-André Taguieff, "Les Métamorphoses idéologiques du racisme et la crise de l'antiracisme" in *Face au racisme*, ed. P. A. Taguieff, vol. 2, *Analyses, hypothèses, perspectives* (Paris: La Découverte, 1991), and several other books and articles published by the same author.

24. Naïr, *Le Regard des vainqueurs*, 232. A similar idea is expressed by Ariane Chebel d'Appolonia in *Les Racismes ordinaires* (Paris: Presse de Sciences Po, 1998). She speaks of a "right to indifference," as opposed, of course, to a "right to difference."

25. Denis Lacorne, *La Crise de l'identité américaine* (Paris: Fayard, 1997). See also the numerous works of Dominique Schnapper.

26. This is precisely the expression used by Roman in "Un Multiculturalisme à la française?"

27. Michel Wieviorka, "Le Multiculturalisme : solution, ou formulation d'un problème?" in *L'Immigration et l'intégration,* ed. Dewitte.

28. Cynthia Ghorra-Gobin, a geographer by specialty, has shown in a recent work on Los Angeles how coalition building has made it possible for a new African American political elite to occupy a strategic place in city politics. She also points out that such coalition politics has its limits, since it allows for the successful integration of only a minority of African Americans, at the expense of many others who remain in poverty and continue to abstain from political participation. See *Los Angeles, le mythe américain inachevé* (Paris: CNRS, 1997). She draws heavily on the work of an American political scientist, Raphael J. Sonenshein, author of *Politics in Black and White: Race and Power in Los Angeles* (Princeton, N.J.: Princeton University Press, 1993).

29. As eminent a sociologist as Dominique Schnapper, who is specialized in questions of citizenship and ethnicity and is widely read in American theories on these subjects, curiously writes that the terms *affirmative action, reverse discrimination,* and *quotas* are all equivalent; see *La Relation à l'Autre*, 326.

30. Pascal Noblet, in *L'Amérique des minorités: Les Politiques d'intégration* (Paris: CIEMI/L'Harmattan, 1993), provides a much better than average description of the actual mechanisms of affirmative action in various contexts, chaps. 5 and 6.

31. Schnapper, *Le Regard de l'autre*, 327–28.

32. Lacorne, *La Crise*, 286.

33. Lacorne, *La Crise*, 328.

34. Lacorne, *La Crise*, 332-33.

35. See, in particular, K. Anthony Appiah and Amy Gutmann, *Color Conscious: The Political Morality of Race* (Princeton, N.J.: Princeton University Press, 1996).

36. See, for example, Manning Marable, *Beyond Black and White: Transforming African American Politics* (New York: Verso, 1995), and Cornel West, *Race Matters* (Boston: Beacon, 1993).

37. In the French literature on ethnicity in U.S. history, one work stands out as a monument: Elise Marienstras's *Les Mythes fondateurs de la nation américaine* (Paris: Maspéro, 1977), since reedited by La Découverte.

38. Lacorne, *La Crise*, 15, and throughout the book.

39. Lacorne, *La Crise*, chaps. 3–6.

40. Lacorne, *La Crise*, chaps. 7–8.

41. New York: Basic Books, 1995.

42. Denis Lacorne, "Pour un multiculturalisme modéré," *Le Débat*, Gallimard 97 (November–December 1997), 163.

43. Lacorne, *La Crise*, 344–45.

44. For Hollinger's developments on the nation and the struggle against social inequality, see *Post-Ethnic America*, chap. 6 ("The Ethnos, the Nation, the World") and the epilogue.

45. See Denis Lacorne, "La Crise de l'identité américaine," *Hérodote* 85 (2d trimester 1997): 18–19. The reference here is to an article that goes by the same title as his book. In the book (343–45), Lacorne remains rather vague about his reasons for being skeptical of Hollinger's postethnic vision; this article provides some additional substantiation for this skepticism.

46. See, for example, John Anner, ed., *Beyond Identity Politics: Emerging Social Justice Movements in Communities of Color* (Boston: South End, 1996).

47. Wacquant, a disciple of both Pierre Bourdieu and William Julius Wilson, is the author of several important articles on different aspects of the U.S. social model, which he compares with the French one. Among his numerous articles, see "Banlieues françaises et ghetto noir américain: De l'amalgame à la comparaison," *French Politics and Society* 10, no. 4 (Fall 1992): 81–102; "Les Pauvres en pâture: La Nouvelle politique de la misère en Amérique," *Hérodote* 85 (2d trimester 1997): 21–33; "La Généralisation de l'insécurité salariale en Amérique: Restructurations d'entreprises et crise de reproduction sociale," *Actes de la recherche en sciences sociales* 115 (December 1996): 65–70; "L'Ascension de l'État pénal en Amérique," *Actes de la recherche en sciences sociales* 124 (September 1998): 7–26.

48. Sophie Body-Gendrot shares with Loïc Wacquant the distinction of knowing both the French and U.S. social models well enough to be able to compare them with some rigor. Among her most important contributions, see especially *Ville et violence: L'Irruption de nouveaux acteurs* (Paris: Presses Universitaires de France, 1993). A more recent work, *Les Villes face à l'insécurité: Des ghettos américains aux banlieues françaises* (Paris: Bayard, 1998), has been the subject of much controversy, having been criticized by Loïc Wacquant, with whom she has formerly coauthored articles, as making too many concessions to the repressive U.S. model of policing. See "Ce vent punitif qui vient d'Amérique," *Le Monde Diplomatique* (April 1999): 1, 24–25.

8

✛

Constitutional Adjudication and Democracy

Comparative Perspectives—The United States, France, and Italy

PASQUALE PASQUINO

The constitutional control of laws enacted by Parliaments is nowadays an essential characteristic of the constitutional state. A large body of juridical literature has been produced in many countries during the last few decades to analyze the modalities of constitutional adjudication. The research project whose preliminary hypotheses I will present here has a slightly different approach from most of the European literature devoted to this topic.

It may be useful to begin with a general *Fragestellung*. The questions I'd like to answer are the following: First, what motivated the constitution-making political classes to introduce in the fundamental law an organ empowered with a control power over the legislature? Second, does the existence of these organs modify the democratic regime, changing its form of government and the theory that tries to make sense of it? Third, is the generalization of organs in charge of constitutional control in the states governed by the rule of law one aspect of a more important phenomenon—the multiplication of state agencies that are not "accountable," so unbound from the political responsibility characterizing elective organs? The role of the elective organs has been so overwhelmingly important in the history of the representative government that we have to ask why next to them the contemporary constitutional states introduced, besides the constitutional courts, independent central banks and so-called independent administrative authorities.

The research methodology employed here is comparative. I would like to start by discussing two quotes. The first one is from a famous (in Italy) article by Vittorio Emanuele Orlando, published in 1951, about the form of government characterizing the Italian constitution enacted in 1948. The central claim of that quote is that the introduction in Italy of a constitutional court—indeed, the first experiment in Europe after the failure of the Austrian *Verfassungsgericht* in the 1920s—would have modified the true nature of the parliamentary democracy, the foundation of which lays in the sovereignty of the Parliament. So, according to Orlando (one of the most famous Italian liberal legal theorists of the century), the new constitution shifted the gravitational center of the political system from the elective assembly to a small group of people, the justices, entrusted with the last word into the legal system.[1]

My second quote comes from the chapter Jürgen Habermas devoted to the role and legitimacy of constitutional adjudication in his last book, *Faktizität und Geltung* (translated with the title *Between Facts and Norms*[2])—more exactly, his conclusion. I propose in this text a different and not normative hypothesis about the role and the rationale of the constitutional courts inside the so-called democratic systems.

Habermas claims that the role and legitimacy of a constitutional court is, or rather ought to be, to watch over the democratic process and "to implement [. . .] democratic procedure and the deliberative form of political opinion- and will-formation" (English ed., 280). This claim makes sense (or possibly not) only inside Habermas's definition of concepts such as democracy and deliberation. I will not delve into the philosophy that leads to those definitions but prefer to start from a plain and quite uncontroversial definition of democracy. Specifically, I will try to show that constitutional adjudication can be understood provided we place it, on the one hand, into a predemocratic tradition—the tradition of moderated or limited government of the eighteenth century—and, on the other hand, into the concrete working of what I'm going to call, with Gustavo Zagrebelsky,[3] the constitutional *Rechtstaat*, which appeared only in the second part of the twentieth century.

CONSTITUTIONAL DEMOCRACY

A sound minimalist definition of a democratic regime is this: "Democracy is a political system in which rulers are appointed by periodically repeated free elections and parties can lose elections."[4]

Nevertheless, such a definition is unable to make sense of a certain number of institutions that characterize most of contemporary so-called democracies or, in my language "constitutional states." Independent authorities, heads of central banks, and members of organs in charge of constitutional control (in the United States, judicial review) are not elected. What matters here is that these officials are not politically responsible to the citizens (a point that had already been clearly stated by the Anti-Federalist Brutus in the debates for the ratification of the American constitution in the state of New York, 1787–88[5]).

Let me focus on that last institution, constitutional courts. No democratic regime after World War II has, to my knowledge, adopted a constitution that entails a "Bulgarian" constitutional court (the Bulgarian one—like Sieyes's *jury constitutionnaire*—was elected). The striking fact is that a constitutional court cannot be considered a subordinate organ/agency when compared with legislative and executive agencies or branches of a contemporary state.

So let me propose the following definition of a constitutional democracy/state (CD/S):

"CD/S is a political system in which the will of an elected majority can be struck down or modified—at least for a while—by a nonelective organ politically not responsible (or by a popular referendum considered inadmissible, as in Italy)."

That definition seems quite startling, and it seems also to conflict with values and beliefs of a parliamentary democracy—so Orlando claimed, at least. If one thinks of the American Supreme Court, the German Bundesverfassungsgericht, or the Italian Corte Costituzionale (the legitimacy of which is absolutely undisputed in the respective public opinions), it is not difficult to agree that these organs have at least two major constitutional competencies:

1. They share with the elected assemblies active legislative power (and not only, as we will see, a negative legislative power, as Kelsen claims[6]).
2. Moreover, they exercise so-called "ordinary constituent power," interpreting and reinterpreting the letter and the spirit of the constitution (in this sense, Brutus's description seems more accurate than the one suggested by Kelsen in 1929).

To avoid misunderstandings, I must stress from the beginning that I do not believe that these organs are supreme or sovereign in any sense of that word: a parliamentary supermajority can always modify the constitution or the power and competencies of a constitutional court (see the Austrian example during the Große Koalition). What I'm claiming here is that they play an extremely important role in almost any state and particularly in any recently established constitutional state so that a theory of democracy that does not take these institutions into account is inevitably incomplete and so partially wrong—wrong like the Newtonian physical theory unable to account for some micro- and macrophenomena. A theory of democracy should also be nowadays a theory of constitutional democracy. That means it should analyze and compare different modalities of constitutional control and try to exhibit the rationale—alternatively the lack of rationale—of those institutions. The starting point for such an inquiry would be in any event the classical doctrine of limited government from the seventeenth and eighteenth centuries (Philip Hunton, Montesquieu, and James Madison).

The major contribution of democratic theory in this century (I'm thinking of Gaetane Mosca, Joseph Schumpeter, and more recently Baron de Manin[7]) is not that in a democratic regime rulers are elected—that we know; it is that in any representative government, elected officials are an elite or, using the Greek words, an oligarchy or aristocracy. Democratic oligarchies are characterized by popular choice of the political elite, so the governing elite needs to be consented; it is not an elite *sui juris*, to use Max Weber's terminology.

Like most contemporary political scientists, I am skeptical about the ability of repeated elections (and connected mechanisms of accountability) to produce "conformity of collective decisions to majority preferences." I do believe, again to avoid misunderstandings, not only that repeated free elections matter but also that they are one of the major institutional procedures that produce both political obligation (for the citizens) and limited power concerning the elites in power, but this is not the same as saying that elections produce accountability or express popular will.

Democracy, to employ older language, is an *Herrschaftsform* (Hermann Heller, Ernest Wolfgang Böckenförde), not a society without *Herrschaft*. Voters have some partial control on representatives. Law obliges citizens, but it is not, pace French constitutional doctrine of the Third Republic (*Carré de Malberg*), popular will. It is just the will of the temporary political majority in the Parliament. Were law identical with popular will, there would be no reason to check the law. But it is not. More checks are needed. Horizontal accountability (some form of checks and balances) has to supplement vertical accountability (electoral principle).

"In framing a government [. . .] you must first enable the government to control the governed [!]; and in the next place oblige it to control itself. A dependence on the people [repeated elections] is, no doubt, the primary control on the government; but experience has taught mankind the necessity of auxiliary precautions" (James Madison, *Federalist Papers*, no. 51). That one of these auxiliary precautions has to take the form of constitutional adjudication is today the central yet mostly disregarded question for a theory of constitutional democracy. A new doctrine of limited government—a postdemocratic, not a predemocratic, one (Montesquieu)—seems to be a central question for contemporary political theory.

THE UNITED STATES

The first form of constitutional control was born about two centuries ago in the United States. At least two characteristics of the American political culture have to be taken into account to understand the early emergence of such an institution.

First, the issue of establishing limited government was paramount among the American Founding Fathers—it is unnecessary to stress the role of Montesquieu on people like James Madison. This effort to avoid any form of "despotism" or "tyranny" (meaning an overwhelming concentration of power on a single state organ—and notably in the legislative agency) led not only to the distribution of power among legislative, executive, and judiciary branches of the central (federal) government but also to the split of political power and competencies between the federal government and the states (we have not forgotten that the states, the old English colonies, preexisted to the American federal constitution and were the true actors of the constitution-making process). For the Founding Fathers, the polyarchical structure of the power was the best guarantee of individual liberty and the only way to create a federal government that would not be the object of criticism by the "republican" Anti-Federalists.

Now, the distribution of competencies between central and local power can generate conflicts among quasi-sovereign different agencies. Hence the necessity to appeal to an umpire able to adjudicate the possible conflicts among the states and the federal government. I need to stress this point since the results of American scholarship about constitutional history[8] have shown clearly the central role that this type of conflict played in the origin and development of judicial review in the American history from the very beginning. Consider, moreover, that federalism has been one of the main reasons to introduce a limited constitutional control in the Weimar Republic (*Staatsgerichtshof*)[9] and that federalism again was one of the arguments forcefully spelled out by Hans Kelsen to justify the introduction of a Verfassungsgericht in the Austrian constitution of 1920.

From this perspective, the role and function of the constitutional court are to maintain the balance inside the polyarchical structure of powers, notably concerning the two quasi-sovereign agencies: states and federal government. Notice that here the constitution is conceived like a mechanism that can keep its self-enforcing equilibrium at the center (Madison, *Federalist Papers,* no. 51) but needs an umpire to avoid the break of the balance between the central political agency and the states (see figure 8.1). Notice, moreover, that the American Supreme Court is appointed by the president with the advice and consent of the Senate, representative of the states.

The second characteristic of American constitutional control is that it is exercised by the judiciary power as such; they speak indeed of judicial review. This is still quite unique today (with the exception of some countries of the British Commonwealth, Canada, Australia, etc., and of the Japanese constitution *octroyée* by McArthur) and has something to do with the American interpretation of the separation of powers, in which the judiciary is in no sense a subordinated power.[10] The locus classicus of such doctrine is the celebrated opinion written in 1803 by Chief Justice Marshall in the case *Marbury v. Madison.* The importance of that opinion lies in the surprising definition of the judiciary (surprising from the European continental point of view). Here we can read:

> It is emphatically the province and duty of the judicial department to say what the law is. Those who apply the rule to particular cases, must of necessity expound and

Figure 8.1

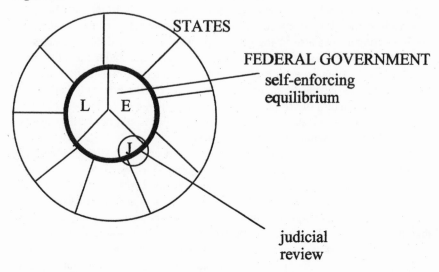

STATES

FEDERAL GOVERNMENT
self-enforcing
equilibrium

judicial
review

interpreter that rule. If two laws [and the U.S. Constitution is a law] conflict with each other, the courts must decide on the operation of each.

So if a law be in opposition to the Constitution; if both the law and the Constitution apply to a particular case, so that the court must either decide that case conformably to the law, disregarding the Constitution; or conformably to the Constitution disregarding the law; the court must determine which of these conflicting rules governs the case. This is of the very essence of judicial duty.

If, then, the courts are to regard the Constitution, and the Constitution is superior to any ordinary act of the legislature, the Constitution, and not such ordinary act, must govern the case to which they both apply.[11]

It was worth quoting this text at length, since although very famous it is not necessary very well known. Not only did Marshall establish the principle of the superiority of the Constitution as "a superior, paramount law, unchangeable by ordinary means," hence "[non]alterable when the legislature shall please to alter it,"[12] he also attributed to the judiciary (i.e., to each court and not only to the Supreme Court) the power to interpret the Constitution to apply or to invalidate statute laws enacted by the elected parliament. Therefore, nonaccountable public officials can nullify the will expressed by the elective organs/agencies.

To understand this point, we need to consider that in the American political culture—by opposition to the French one—statutes passed by Congress are not the only source of law (in the large sense of this word = *droit, Recht*); jurisprudence is a concurrent source, so that we can say that the tradition of common law produced in the first constitutional state with a rigid constitution what we call judicial review. Judges and representatives are coordinate figures. And the mistrust against the democratic-elective organs typical of eighteenth-century liberalism (remember the issue of tyranny of majority, which plays such an important role for James Madison) makes plain, besides the federal structure, the early emergence of judicial review in America.

EUROPE

The American judicial review has been a long-lasting exception and an unique institution among constitutional systems. Only after World War II—let alone the wrecked attempt in Austria—did organs exercising a similar role spread widely in the new constitutional states. The German Bundesverfassungsgericht became functional in 1951, the Italian Constitutional Court in 1956, and the French Conseil Constitutionnel in 1958, although it became really active only after 1974, for reasons I'll consider later. Different issues have to be addressed concerning those state organs: first, the reason for the long European resistance to constitutional adjudication; second, the type of conflicts they judge; third, how they are put in motion, since they are subject to the juridical principle of "passivity" (they cannot put themselves in motion); and finally, the complex and sometimes different roles of constitutional adjudication in the different countries.

Let me start with the first matter. The major obstacle on the European continent to the establishment of an organ empowered with constitutional control has been what I call the "French ideology"—more precisely, the idea that in the representative government the Parliament is the only organ legitimate to express popular will. As Carré de Malberg, the most prominent law theorist of the French Third Republic used to say, the law (i.e., the will of the Parliament) is the only true expression of general will. Since the general will is a sovereign power, it would be useless and in any event preposterous to check the sovereign.[13] As in the old monarchy, so in the parliamentary democracy the sovereign cannot be wrong. This idea of the embodiment of the popular will in the elective organs was strenuously advocated by the Italian communist party (and notably by Togliatti) in the Italian Constituent Assembly of 1946–47, which notwithstanding the communist democratic opposition decided to establish a constitutional court supported by a majority of Catholics and liberals. It is an irony of history that the same principle that identifies democracy with direct elections is nowadays the firmest tenet of the most conservative Italian political party, Alleanza Nazionale!

The privilege of democratic elective institutions that monopolize political power is certainly the main reason for the long resistance of the continental political systems to any constitutional control. If you look for more evidence, you may read the answer given by Carré de Malberg to Hans Kelsen when the Austrian legal theorist went to Paris in 1928 to present his model of constitutional court. The debate between the Austrian and the French theorist was published in the Annuaire de l'Institut International de Droit Public in 1929.

The conflicts presented to the constitutional courts are essentially of three types: conflicts among state organs, conflicts between central government and *Länder*[14] (where there is a federal structure), and, eventually, conflicts among statute laws and in same cases acts of the administration, on one side, and the constitution, on the other. The constitution is not only a mechanism attributing and distributing competencies among a plurality of organs that ought not to be modified to avoid despotism (I mean by this word the concentration of too much power in a single branch or agency, as in the classical eighteenth-century doctrine). The constitution is also a set of values and principles superior to the ordinary law since they cannot be modified by the simple majority that may do and undo statute laws. In other words, constitutional norms are "superstable" (more stable than stable laws) because they can be modified only by a supermajority. The constitution in the doctrine and in the reality of the twentieth century (at least where constitution matters) incorporates a special degree of *Rechtsicherheit*.

We should consider more precisely this idea of the constitution as a norm and not as a simple mechanism (I owe this distinction to Michel Troper, who used it in a different context[15]). But first let me remind you that any constitutional court is subject to the principle of "passivity." That means in the juridical language that no court can act *motu proprio*; unlike the executive or the legislative power, it can only answer to a question asked by another actor in the juridical system. The concrete consequence of that principle is that it is extremely important to consider who are the actors constitutionally authorized to appeal the organ in charge of constitutional adjudication. In general, contemporary constitutions admit one or more of the following four actors: (1) ordinary citizens (*recurso de amparo, Verfassungsbeschwerde*), (2) lower courts (judges and sometimes litigants in a trial), (3) state organs or *Länder* (in federal systems), and (4) the minority of representative assemblies (e.g., France since 1974). These varying opportunities for admittance play a major role in shaping the political and constitutional system.

We can distinguish basically among cases such as France, where the political class has been very keen up to today to keep the monopoly of the *saisine* (referral to the Constitutional Council); Italy, where the judiciary power has maintained a monopoly; and Germany, where about 90 percent of the appeals to the Federal Constitutional Court are initiated by citizens (i.e., by lawyers).

Let me spell out some differences. The French case is quite peculiar and deserves to be considered more accurately. The Conseil Constitutionnel was introduced by the Fifth Republic because General de Gaulle wanted to have an option of last resort to veto the Parliament (i.e., the political parties). In fact, until 1974 the Conseil Constitutionnel could be appealed only by the president of the republic, the first minister, and the presidents of the two representative assemblies. It was only in 1974 that a much less powerful president than de Gaulle, Giscard d'Estaing, proposed a reform of the mechanism of appeal/referral (the *saisine*) giving the minority the possibility to appeal the Council against a law voted by the majority before its official promulgation. The promulgated law is still in French, however, and cannot be nullified!

The reasons as well as the context of that reform are extremely important. Giscard was probably the first to realize that the French constitutional system of the Fifth Republic could put the president in a weak and difficult position if the minority would have won the legislative elections during his term. Remember that the French parliament is elected every five years and the presidential terms lasts seven, and remember that Giscard won the presidential elections in 1974 against Mitterrand with a very slim majority. So his idea was to give the minority the possibility to put a potential veto on the laws passed by the majority, avoiding the constant appeal by the president to the Council if he became the first president to experience the "cohabitation." It is clear that to do that he had to give this opportunity to the actual minority (the socialists), but this is the inescapable logic of any system based on changeover of political power between parties.

Consider again the definition I gave of a democratic regime: a political system in which the governing party(ies) can (and will inevitably at some point) lose the elections. Because in the contemporary *Parteienstaaten* there is no possible balance between legislative and executive power, since the latter is the expression of the parliamentary majority and since the majority knows that after a while (months or years) it will became the minority, it is sensible to introduce a mechanism that can or should preclude those who lose the election will lose everything.[16] The elections are not a divine judgment that sends the loser to hell. They simply give to the winners a fraction of political power they will use under the control of an umpire who can be asked to pass his judgment if the minority requests it.

Institutions have their own life, so they do not necessarily comply with the intentions of the framers. The knowledge of those intentions does not give us much more than the knowledge of the intentions—the tautology comes from the methodological individualism, not from me. Look at the Italian case, which also is quite peculiar and intriguing. Nowhere outside the United States (and some countries of the British Commonwealth) did any constitution (one should say any political class) dare to attribute to the judiciary as such the constitutional adjudication; everywhere else that function has been assigned to a special agency independent from the three branches of the traditional separation of powers. The reasons for the introduction by the Constituent Assembly in 1947 of the Corte Costituzionale (whose members are appointed by the Parliament, the president, and the high courts) are well known, and they do not differ substantially from the reasons that explain the French reform of 1974. The Christian Democrats were quite anxious about the possibility that the next legislative elections in 1948 would have produced a social-communist majority in the Parliament. So they thought that a nonelective body made up of legal people would have been a possible guarantee against a too progressive and anti-Catholic legislation.[17] The conservative stand of most of the Italian lawyers and magistrates after World War II was, at that point, not in question. However, the choice to give the judiciary the monopoly of referral (*impugnativa*) to the Constitutional Court eventually produced an unexpected consequence. Slowly but inevitably, the connection between the court and the ordinary judges ended up in the establishment of a counterpower that is the only one able to check the political class in the Italian constitutional system.

So, even though the Italian Court is an agency outside the judiciary as such, the mechanism of referral monopolized by the ordinary judges has made the constitutional adjudication in Italy quite similar, notwithstanding its centralized character, to the American judicial review. This is a sort of anomaly in the European context of the separation of powers that may not entirely survive the actual constitutional reform. It is worth noting that in the draft presented in September 2000 by the bicameral committee in charge of the revision of the constitution, the proposal was made to open the referral to the court by the members of Parliament, which at the same time possibly protects the minority in a majoritarian system and serves as a way to break the monopoly of the judiciary.

It may be interesting to look more precisely at the working and ideology of the Italian constitutional adjudication. If the French Constitutional Council is a sort of nonelective third chamber whose role is essentially to maintain the balance between the majority and the minority—Mauro Cappelletti used some years ago the expression of "political control" to characterize the French constitutional adjudication[18]—the Italian and the German courts stress their function of protection of individual rights. The central idea as it has been presented recently by the justice Gustavo Zagrebelsky[19] can be summed up in the following way: The court is an organ of jurisdiction that stands above and beyond political dynamics (22). Its function consists of putting the law (*il diritto*) above politics, so that *lex facit legem* and not *rex facit legem*. That the *rex* or the sovereign be democratically elected does not change the need to put the rule of law above the rule of men (23). Politics is not the last word. There are principles of justice written down in most of the contemporary constitutions that are superior to the statutes and that the legislator must obey.

So far so good. Even in France no political majority can claim that it is right from the juridical point of view since it is politically majoritarian. But this is just the beginning of the story. The constitutionalization of principles of justice—in other words, the fact that a constitution no longer is a simple mechanism regulating the relationships among powers and state agencies to avoid despotism and to guarantee moderation and limited government but rather a set of norms with ethical content and sometimes even programmatic value—opens a huge set of problems that are at the core of constitutional adjudication. To use Zagrebelsky's terms, these principles embodied in the fundamental law "are different and it may be that contradictions appear" (33). For instance, the principle of liberty and equality may conflict; now "the role of the Constitutional Court is to check that these different principles of justice are respected by the statute laws in a way compatible with the constitution" (35). More important, Zagrebelsky explicitly says that constitutional control has nothing to do with a practical syllogism that has been for two centuries (starting with Condorcet and Kant) the model of the jurisdictional activity in European culture. The court does not make syllogisms; it has "to compose the pluralism of constitutional values in the most sensible way" (36) (the principle of sensibility/*ragionevolezza*), and it has to reformulate and actualize the compromise of values proper to any constitution.

To make this point more concretely understandable, consider the following example. An American young girl was adopted by a Neapolitan family a couple of years ago. After more than a year, the court was informed and would have had to take the girl away from the family in application of a statute law that states it is forbidden in Italy to adopt a baby if the father is more than forty years older than the baby. Now, since the father was forty years and two months older than the girl, and since she was well integrated in the new family, the judge resisted applying the law, arguing for an exception of unconstitutionality of the law, and sent the case to the supreme court. The constitutional court made a very peculiar decision quite typical of its way of working. The justices did not strike down the law in its entirety, for it seemed quite sensible indeed, but they modified it, claiming that the ordinary judge can at his discretion depart from the law in special cases and only in the child's interest. So the statute law was changed, introducing a discretionary power for the judge who must apply it to concrete cases. This example shows two things. On one hand, the principle of generality of law can by relaxed in the interest of the superior value of justice—this reminds us of the old Aristotelian concept of *epieikeia*, claiming that justice can be done acting contra and extra *legem*. On the other hand, the court acts as a true colegislator, which does not simply nullify statutes that contradict the text of the constitution but redefines the content itself of the legislation.

It would be interesting to consider also another peculiar power of the Italian court, which has been the object of a large debate during the last months: the possibility to declare unconstitutional an abrogative referendum. That implies the Corte Costituzionale can control not only the will of an elected Parliament but also the so-called popular will. For now, however, I will leave this question unaddressed.

CONCLUSION

If we consider the role and the importance of the organs in charge of constitutional adjudication in contemporary states, two possibilities are open to political theory:

1. Redefine the concept of democracy, disentangling it from the "majoritarian premise" or, in my language, from the electoral principle.
2. Develop a doctrine of the constitutional state in which democracy is an important value but not the only one we care about and not necessarily the one we care about the most.

It is not surprising that I prefer the second path since as a European, I know that constitutional control is a very recent institution that has modified the democratic regime. On the other hand, it is perfectly understandable that American thinkers such as Ronald Dworkin in his last book[20] choose the other way, rejecting, as American history consistently did, the "connection between democracy and majority will." Nonetheless, we are left with the question as to why (except for rhetorical reasons, such as "Democratic is beautiful" or "Everything good is democratic") we should deduce the totality of the institutions of a constitutional state and their legitimacy from a single principle and not from more than one.

NOTES

1.

The creation of the Constitutional Court [. . .] contains an underlying doubtful compatibility with the traditional form of parliamentary democracy; I mean to say that the existence and the way in which is formed an authority whose main figure is that of being super-parliamentary. The very fact that the Parliament would no longer be sovereign, but would be subject to a sort of subordination vis-à-vis another authority, seems to me to shift the gravitational center of the political system [emphasis added]. It will be said that the competence of the high court will be rigidly confined to resolving points of law in a purely objective fashion. Yet who can believe in a total separation between law and fact? [. . .] What is certain is that the last word on vital government issues will no longer be left to the elective Assemblies, but to eight people [which is the majority of the fifteen justices].

("Studio sulla forma di governo vigente in Italia secondo la Costituzione del 1948," *Rivista trimestrale di diritto pubblico* 1 [1951]: 5–45, 43)

2. Cambridge Mass.: MIT Press, 1996.

3. *Il diritto mite* (Torino: Einaudi, 1992).

4. A. Przeworski, *Democracy and the Market* (New York: Cambridge University Press, 1991), 10; see also A. Przeworski, "Minimalist Conception of Democracy: A Defense," paper prepared for a conference on "Rethinking Democracy for a New Century," Yale University, 28 February–2 March 1997.

5. "Had the construction of the constitution been left with the legislature, they would have explained it at their peril; if they exceed their powers, or sought to find, in the spirit of the constitution, more than was expressed in the letter, the people from whom they derived their power could remove them, and do themself right" (essay 15, 20 March 1788, *The Anti-Federalist Papers and the Constitutional Convention Debates*, ed. R. Ketcham [New York: Mentor, 1986], 309).

6. See G. Parodi, *La sentenza additiva a dispositivo generico* (Torino, Giappichelli, 1996).

7. *Principes du gouvernement représentatif* (Paris: Calmann-Lévy, 1995).

8. See, notably, J. N. Rakove, "The Origins of Judicial Review: A Plea for New Contexts," *Stanford Law Review* 49 (1996–97): 1031–64.

9. Although under the restrictive clause that "Reichsrecht bricht Landesrecht"; what is not the case in the United States is where the constitutional adjudication may protect state legislation against the federal statutes and vice versa. See, respectively, Garcia and Lopez.

10. See P. Pasquino, *Uno e trino* (Milano: Anabasi, 1994).
11. *Marbury v. Madison*, I Crunch 137 (1803).
12. Article 5 of the U.S. Constitution introduced a very cumbersome mechanism to pass constitutional amendments.
13. This thesis was clearly stated more than thirty years ago by Carlo Lavagna:

> There is a whole theory of the sovereignty of the popular will both in French and in Marxist ideology, which both oppose checks. This is because, starting from the notion that the representatives of the people enjoy absolute sovereignty and that everything they do they do well by the mere fact that they are the sovereign, checking the activity of the sovereign would be senseless or even constitute a limitation of the people's sovereignty. On the other hand, we know that the sovereignty of these supreme state organs is an abstraction. In actual fact, they are made up of political groups that work according to given needs and according to majority guidelines which may not always conicide with constitutional rules. Hence the need for further mechanisms rather than simply relying on the goodwill of legislators and government leaders. Yet, these same sovereign political forces have taken care to introduce mechanisms to safeguard the constitution that they themselves have devised, to protect their own ideologies, above all in relation to the succession of power to opposite, heterogeneous political forces.

(*Le costituzioni rigide: Corso di diritto costituzionale e comparato.* Lezioni tenute nell'anno accademico 1963–64 [Rome: Edizioni Ricerche, 1964], 241).
14. I'm going to use the German word to designate the political subunits to avoid the American state, which produces some confusion in the European ear.
15. M. Troper, "L'Expérience américaine et la Constitution française du 3 septembre 1791", in *Constitution & Revolution*, Macerata, Laboratorio di storia costituzionale (1995): 225–38.
16. During the debates that led to the reform of 1974, Jean Lecanuet, minister of justice, developed the following argument: "Imagine that one day we [the majority] were to regret not having created a free institution, set over and above all other powers and able to adjudicate the constitutionality of the laws; imagine one day . . . that means the day we [the conservative majority] will be the opposition!" Quoted by D. Rousseau, *Droit du contentieux constitutionnel* (Paris: Montchrestien, 1993), 64, fn. 24.
17. See F. Rigano, *Costituzione e potere giudiziario: La Corte Costituzionale, "argine" contro la sinistra nel disegno democristiano* (Padova: Cedam, 1982), 231*ff*.
18. *Judicial Review in the Contemporary World* (Indianapolis: Bobbs-Merrill, 1971), 2*ff*.
19. "I problemi costituzionali in Italia," lecture given at Bergamo, 22 March 1997, Accademia della Guardia di Finanza, Ufficio addestramento e studi.
20. *Freedom's Law* (Cambridge, Mass.: Harvard University Press, 1996).

Index

About the Contributors

Catherine Audard is a Visiting Fellow at the London School of Economics, where she teaches philosophy. She is the cofounder and the present chair of the Forum for European Philosophy, based at the London School of Economics. Her current concerns are moral issues in political theory, conceptions of citizenship in France, multiculturalism, and deliberative democracy. Her most recent book is *Anthologie historique et critique de l'utilitarisme* in three volumes (Presses Universitaires de France, 1999). She has coedited *Individu et justice sociale* (Le Seuil, 1988) and has edited *Le Respect* (Autrement, 1993). She has also published numerous articles on utilitarianism, liberalism, justice, and citizenship in various journals and collections. She has translated into French John Rawls's *Theory of Justice* (Le Seuil, 1987), *Political Liberalism* (Presses Universitaires de France, 1995), and a collection of Rawls's earlier papers under the title *Justice et démocratie* (Le Seuil, 1993). She has recently published a new French translation of J. S. Mill's *Utilitarianism* (Presses Universitaires de France, 1998). She is currently finishing a book on *Citoyenneté et individualité morale*.

Benjamin R. Barber is Walt Whitman Professor of Political Science at Rutgers University, where he directs the Walt Whitman Center for the Culture and Politics of Democracy. Barber brings an abiding concern for democracy and citizenship to issues of politics, culture, and education both in America and abroad. He consults regularly with political and educational leaders in the United States and Europe, including former President Clinton and the German government. Barber's fourteen books include the classic *Strong Democracy* (University of California Press, 1984), as well as the novel *Marriage Voices* (Simon & Schuster, 1981) and with Patrick Watson the prize-winning CBC/PBS ten-part television series *The Struggle for Democracy*. In addition to his best-selling *Jihad versus McWorld* (Ballantine, 1996, paperback, translated into ten languages), his latest books include *A Place for Us: How to make Society Civil and Democracy Strong* (Farrar, Strauss, 1998), *A Passion for Democracy* (Princeton University Press, 1998), and the forthcoming *My Affair with Clinton: An Intellectual Memoir* (Norton, 2001).

James A. Cohen is a professor of political science at the University of Paris–VIII (Saint-Denis) and a lecturer at the Institut d'études politiques de Paris and the Institut des hautes études de l'Amérique Latine. He works on issues of citizenship and ethnicity in Europe and North America as well as questions of democracy and development in Latin America and the Caribbean. He is a contributor to the collective volume *Immigration et integration: L'État des savoirs* (La Decouverte, 1999) and a frequent contributor to the journal *Hommes et migrations*. He has also edited the collective volume *Amérique latine: Démocratie et exclusion* (L'Harmattan, 1994).

Frank Cunningham is professor of philosophy and Principal of Innis College at the University of Toronto. Among his books are *Democratic Theory and Socialism* (Cambridge University Press, 1987), *The Real World of Democracy Revisited* (Humanities Press, 1994), and *Democratic Theories: A Critical Introduction* (Routledge, 2000). A book is in preparation for Rowman & Littlefield on the political thought of C. B. Macpherson. He is past president of the Canadian Philosophical Association.

Omar Dahbour teaches philosophy at Hunter College of the City University of New York. He is coeditor of *The Nationalism Reader* (1995), editor of *Philosophical Perspectives on National Identity* (a special issue of *The Philosophical Forum*, 1996–97), and author of articles or reviews on self-determination, national identity, and other topics in the *Journal of the History of Philosophy*, *History of European Ideas*, *Canadian Journal of Philosophy*, *Theory and Society*, *German Politics and Society*, and other publications.

Carol C. Gould is professor of philosophy at Stevens Institute of Technology, research associate at the Centre de Recherche en Epistemologie Appliquée, École Polytechnique, Paris, and adjunct professor of International and Public Affairs at Columbia University. In 2000–01, she was Fulbright Florence Chair of Political and Social Science at the European University Institute in Fiesole, Italy and a Fellow at the Woodrow Wilson Center for Scholars in Washington, D.C. She is the author of *Marx's Social Ontology* (MIT Press, 1978) and *Rethinking Democracy* (Cambridge University Press, 1988); editor or coeditor of five previous books, including *Women and Philosophy* (with Marx W. Wartofksy); *Beyond Domination: New Perspectives on Women and Philosophy*, *The Information Web: Ethical and Social Implications of Computer Networking*, and most recently *Gender* (Humanity/Prometheus Books, 1999). She has also published more than forty articles in social and political philosophy, applied ethics, and feminist philosophy. She is currently co–executive director of the Society for Philosophy and Public Affairs and past president of the American Society of Value Inquiry.

Christopher W. Morris is professor of philosophy at Bowling Green State University. He has recently been visiting research fellow in philosophy at the University of Amsterdam and a visiting scholar in politics at New York University. He is also a research associate at Centre de Recherche en Epistemologie Appliquée, École Polytechnique, Paris. His recent publications include *An Essay on the Modern State* (Cambridge University Press, 1998), *The Social Contract Theorists: Critical Essays on Hobbes, Locke, and Rousseau* (Rowman & Littlefield, 1999), and *Rational Commitment and Social Justice: Essays for Gregory Kavka*, coedited with Jules L. Coleman (Cambridge University Press, 1998).

Pasquale Pasquino is director of research at the Centre Nationale de la Recherche Scientifique, Paris, and a Visiting Professor of law and politics at New York University. He is the author of four books, including *Thomas Hobbes, Stato di natura e libertà civile* (Anabasi, 1994) and *Sieyes et l'invention de la constitution* (Editions Odile Jacob, 1998), and of more than fifty articles on German and French political and constitutional theory, and the theme of order and threat in early modern political theory.